ENJOYING
BIRDS IN HAWAII

A Birdfinding Guide to the Fiftieth State

ALSO BY H. DOUGLAS PRATT

A Field Guide to the Birds of Hawaii and the Tropical Pacific
(with Phillip L. Bruner and Delwyn G. Berrett; illustrated by Pratt)
Princeton University Press, 1987

Voices of Hawaii's Birds
(Cassette tapes and accompanying text)
Hawaii Audubon Society; expected late 1993

The Hawaiian Honeycreepers
Oxford University Press; work in progress, publication date open

Numerous Scientific Papers in
The Condor, Wilson Bulletin, The Auk, Western Birds, 'Elepaio, Micronesica,
and other journals

Popular articles and illustrations in
*Audubon , Birding , American Birds, Defenders, National Wildlife, Scientific
News,* and other magazines.

A Field Guide to the Birds of North America
(one quarter of color plates by Pratt)
National Geographic Society, 1983, 1987

Forest Bird Communities of the Hawaiian Islands
(by J. M. Scott and a team of ornithologists; illustrated by Pratt)
Cooper Ornithological Society Studies in Avian Biology No. 9, 1986

Birds of Colonial Williamsburg
(by Alan Feduccia; featuring 72 bird portraits by Pratt)
Colonial Williamsburg Foundation, 1989

Birds of the Blue Ridge Mountains
(by Marcus B. Simpson; illustrated by Pratt)
University of North Carolina Press, 1992

ENJOYING
BIRDS IN
HAWAII

A Birdfinding Guide to the Fiftieth State

BY H. DOUGLAS PRATT, PH. D.
PAINTINGS, MAPS, AND
PHOTOGRAPHS BY THE AUTHOR.

MUTUAL PUBLISHING

LCC 91-067618

Design
Michael Horton Design

Imagesetting
Femar Graphics

First Printing 1993
1 2 3 4 5 6 7 8 9

ISBN 0-935180-00-1

Mutual Publishing
1127 11th Avenue, Mezz. B
Honolulu, Hawaii 96816
Telephone (808) 732-1709
Fax (808) 734-4094

Printed in Australia

To
Robert L. Pyle

TABLE OF CONTENTS

FOREWORD

Island birds are special. Worldwide, island species are often the most unusual members of their families. The more isolated the island group, the more its birds stand apart from their continental ancestors. Hawaii's birds are special indeed because these islands are the world's most isolated archipelago. From any direction, birds have to cross at least 2,500 miles of open sea to reach the larger islands. Over the eons only a few small land birds have done so, and even fewer have come in large enough numbers to colonize. Scientists estimate that only one colonizer succeeded every 100,000 years! These few were the ancestors of all of Hawaii's native land birds. Seabirds and waterfowl could make the sea crossing more easily, and some found these isolated, predator-free islands ideal nesting grounds. Likewise, shorebirds could easily reach the islands, but few of them became residents. Instead, they became annual winter visitors to what is still regarded as an earthly paradise. And what an avian paradise it must have been! With no ground-dwelling predators such as mammals and snakes (which could not make the ocean crossing), birds no longer had to fly to survive and many became flightless. Likewise bird diseases were left behind on the continents, along with vectors such as mosquitoes that might have spread diseases from migrants. Because the successful colonizers left behind their competitors, they were free to change in ways that would not have been possible in their ancestral homes. Many new species evolved as birds successively colonized the different islands. Thus was built up a unique native avifauna. But the very factors that made the Hawaiian Islands such a brave new avian world for birds also left the birds vulnerable to subsequent changes.

About 10,000 years ago, mankind first discovered the Hawaiian Islands. These Polynesian explorers brought with them not only the seeds of their food plants, but the seeds of destruction as well. The Polynesians brought chickens, dogs, pigs, and, unintentionally, rats. The first Hawaiians made short work of the defenseless flightless birds and burned off the native forest to make way for agriculture. By the late 1700s, almost all of the lowlands of the main islands were under cultivation. Nearly half the bird species that evolved in the islands had by then perished. We know of their existence only from recently discovered subfossil remains.

But the Polynesian settlers were only the first part of a one-two human punch. The arrival of Captain James Cook in 1778 brought the islands to the attention of the outside world for the first time, and new changes were swift in coming. Habitat destruction continued apace, and extended further up into the mountains. Alien plants and animals proved in all too many cases to be weeds and pests. European diseases decimated the native Hawaiian people and the introduction of mosquitoes by a spiteful ship captain in the 1820s provided a vector for avian diseases that would do the same to the birds. By the mid-19th Century, the lowlands of Oahu were so devoid of songbirds that appeals went out to travellers to bring back foreign birds for introduction. Then, around the turn of the 20th Century, birds began to disappear mysteriously from seemingly untouched forests on the neighbor islands. Whole species were swept away in a sudden wave of extinction. Epizootic disease is thought to have been the culprit, partly because it would explain the rapidity of the catastrophe and partly because distributions of surviving species today seem to be determined by the presence or absence of disease-carrying mosquitoes. These insects are found mostly in the lowlands up to about 4,000 ft. and native birds are rarely found below that elevation, even in seemingly pristine native forests.

Following the turn-of-the-century declines, Hawaii's birds entered a period of relative tranquility. Rare species did not necessarily recover, but neither did any further species become extinct until about 1970. In fact, several species thought to be extinct were "rediscovered" in the 1950s and 1960s. Now, as the 21st Century approaches, Hawaii's avifauna seems poised for a new wave of extinctions already begun with the loss of the Kauai Oo in the late 1980s. Over half of the birds on the Federal List of Endangered Species are Hawaiian. The cumulative burden of modern mankind's various offenses against the environment are proving intolerable for sensitive relict species such as the Poo-uli. The time to observe and study Hawaii's native birds is now. The more people see and appreciate Hawaii's birds, the more they will support efforts to save them. Hawaii's rare native birds have for too long been "out of sight, out of mind." When a California Condor chick hatches, we see it on the network news, but when the last Kauai Oo disappeared, it hardly warranted a footnote. Perhaps this guide will help to increase awareness of this special Hawaiian legacy among both residents and visitors.

The value of increased attention notwithstanding, birders must realize that they must do nothing to exacerbate the problems. Adding a bird to one's life list is not worth contributing to its demise! Nest sites of critically endangered species must remain sacrosanct. Disturbances such as helicopter flights must be kept to a minimum. No one should hike into a wilderness area without cleaning his or her clothing and footwear of weed seeds. Restrictions on entry into sensitive areas are not unreasonable, as most birders will realize. And fortunately, virtually all the species one can reasonably expect to see can be found, as this guide will show, without undue disturbance.

Hawaii's avifauna today reflects an environment that is totally altered by the actions of human beings. Nevertheless, it is still a fascinating avian community from which much can be learned. Not every story about Hawaiian birds is a tragedy. Even some remnants of nearly pristine Hawaiian habitat can be found if you know where to look; this book will lead you to some of them. The birds in Hawaii today can provide the birder with challenges, surprises, and enjoyment. As a major "migrant trap" Hawaii has tremendous potential for producing birds new to the AOU Check-list area. Because many remote areas are seldom visited by competent observers, and because there are so many potential discoveries, birders even have the chance to rediscover a supposedly extinct species. Even without winning the birding lottery in that fashion, you will find birding in the Hawaiian Islands to be as exciting as any. I hope this guide contributes to that excitement.

Acknowledgements

I could not list all of the many people who, over the years, have helped me in so many ways to learn about Hawaiian birds. Some clearly deserve a special word of thanks, and I apologize to any I have overlooked. Phil Bruner, a valued collaborator and field companion, and his wife Andrea introduced me to Hawaiian birds in 1974 and remain among my closest friends. Others who have provided hospitality and field assistance include Delwyn and Francine Berrett, Terry Casey, Sheila Conant, Regi and Susan David, C. J. and Carol Ralph, and Rob and Annarie Shallenberger. Those who have helped me gain access to restricted areas or have shared special knowledge include Tonnie Casey, Mark Collins, Jon Giffin, Vicki Grieve, Jim Jacobi, Cameron Kepler, Jaan Lepson, Dan Moriarty, Stephen Mountainspring, J. Michael Scott, John Sincock, Lani Stemmermann, Charles van Riper III, Ron Walker, Rick Warshauer, Dick Wass, Mark White, and David W. Woodside. I thank John Oney, former Director of the Cincinnati Nature Center, for teaching me the tour leading business, and Dave Blanton of Voyagers International for keeping me active in it. Fellow birders Regi David, Peter Donaldson, Bill Eley, David Kuhn, and Fred Zeillemaker have shared their knowledge and discoveries with me. This book is dedicated to Robert L. Pyle, the reigning "champion birder" of Hawaii (the only person to have seen over 200 species in the state), who has been a constant source of information and encouragement. As Regional Editor for *American Birds* and Curatorial Assistant in Ornithology at the Bishop Museum, he has cheerfully assisted visiting birders for years.

H. Douglas Pratt
Museum of Natural Science
Louisiana State University
Baton Rouge, Louisiana 70803-3216

HOW TO USE THIS BOOK

SCOPE AND PURPOSE

This guide is intended to be an aid to both resident and visiting birders in the main Hawaiian Islands (The Northwestern Hawaiian Islands are not included; they are largely uninhabited and visits are by special permit only). It is *not* a field guide; for identifying birds, one should consult any of several good references (see Field Guides under Birding Tips, below). Instead this book will tell you where to go for the best birding as well as where to find particular species that you may want to see. In addition, the text includes information not directly related to birds that will enhance the birder's enjoyment of the Hawaiian experience. For example, localities are included that almost everyone will visit, but which may not have special significance to the birder. Also, bits of historical and ecological information are given that will enable the birder to better appreciate the birds and their habitats. I emphasize the conservation of native birds and the need for further efforts to insure their long-term survival. Over half the birds on the Federal List of Endangered Species are Hawaiian, yet the amount of attention and funding devoted to them is disproportionately small.

ORGANIZATION

The book is divided into three major sections: an **Introduction** includes general information about birds and birding in Hawaii; **The Site Guide** covers the most important birding localities island-by-island; and **The Species Guide** tells where you have the best chance of finding a particular bird. In addition, a section titled **For Further Information** provides a supplemental reading and reference list, and an **Appendix** gives a photographic guide to plants of importance to birders in Hawaii. The three main sections are discussed in more detail below.

Introduction. This section will introduce you to the major groups of birds found in Hawaii and special problems they present to the observer. Also, you will find information about the major avian habitats and how to recognize them. Every successful birder has to know a little botany and ecology. This section also gives practical hints about equipment and reference books you will need as well as information about travel in the islands from the birder's perspective (the kind of information the standard tourist brochures leave out). In addition, there is a discussion of organized birding tours and how to choose a good one.

The Site Guide. This section is divided into five parts, one for each of the main islands of Oahu, Molokai, Maui, Hawaii (often referred to as the Big Island), and Kauai. Each part begins with a map of the island with birding localities numbered. A brief discussion of the island as a whole follows, and a list of the island's most widespread and common birds (seasonally common species are indicated by an asterisk) is given. These are species that virtually anyone will see without any special effort. They are generally ignored in the discussions of individual sites. The site accounts are organized as follows: the **Location** section is just that, with reference to surrounding areas; the **Access** section gives more specific directions for getting to the site as well as information on how to obtain permission (when necessary) to enter the site; **Precautions** are given where appropriate; and a list of **Notable Species** is given. The last is not to be taken as a complete list; it includes only those of special interest, with the most notable ones boldfaced. A general discussion about the site and its birds concludes the account. Detail maps are presented throughout The Site Guide where needed. Some of these include more than one numbered locality. In addition the five island divisions, The Site Guide includes a section that discusses pelagic birding.

　　The Species Guide. This is a species-by-species discussion of particularly good places to find birds of special interest. Very common or widespread birds are not included; no one needs to be told where to see a Common Myna! To avoid repetition, some accounts simply refer the reader to numbered localities in The Site Guide. A few species are most easily found in places not included in The Site Guide (usually because the locality is good only for those species). In such cases, detailed directions are included in the species account.

LEARNING A LITTLE HAWAIIAN

　　Anyone who visits the Hawaiian Islands is immediately aware of the all-pervasive influence of the Hawaiian language. Although only a few people in a few isolated places now speak Hawaiian on a daily basis, it lives on in songs, place names, and bird names as well as in its heavy influence on the English now spoken in Hawaii and elsewhere. Words such as *aloha, lei, lanai, kane,* and *wahine* have long been found in English dictionaries. Now, such local terms as *mauka, makai, kama'aina , kipuka,* and *haole* are so widely used and understood by all ethnic groups in Hawaii that they are considered English words and are included as such in, for example, the Second Edition of the *Random House Dictionary of the English Language (Unabridged)* (1987, Random House, New York). No one can spend any time in Hawaii without learning at least a few such terms, but birders are particularly aware of the Hawaiian influence because the English names of native birds are, for the most part, based on the original Hawaiian. Your enjoyment of birding in Hawaii will be greatly enhanced if you take a little time to learn to pronounce Hawaiian words (it's not as difficult as some people seem to think) and to learn their meanings. Of course, a thorough discussion of Hawaiian pronunciation is far beyond the scope of this guide but these few comments may help you get started on the right track. An excellent recorded guide to pronunciation of place names and other everyday Hawaiian words, *Is it Hawai'i or Havai'i?,* a cassette tape by Keith Haugen, is available at bookstores in the islands or from Island Viking, P. O. Box 1976, Honolulu, HI 96805.

　　Hawaiian consonants are pronounced exactly as in English except for w, which is sometimes pronounced as a soft v. The v-sound is frequently overdone. The rule is w-sound after o or u or initially, v-sound after i or e, either way after a (this is usually a matter of custom and is rather arbitrary). Hawaiian vowels are the same as those in Romance languages such as Italian or Spanish. Hawaiian orthography also uses a "letter" that is not in the English alphabet. You probably noticed it in the word *kamaʻaina* in the previous paragraph. The upside down apostrophe is called a glottal stop. It represents a stoppage of sound between two vowels as in the English interjection "uh-oh." Unfortunately, English speakers misinterpreted it as a mark of punctuation rather than a letter and left it out when they borrowed Hawaiian words. That produced words with long unbroken series of vowels that can be rather bewildering to the novice. With the glottal stops included, they are not so daunting. (Incidentally, when you see a glottal stop at the start of a word, it just means that, in a sentence, there would be a glottal stop between the previous word, which would always end in a vowel, and that one.) The glottal stop also helps to distinguish the diphthongs *ei, eu, oi, ou, ai, ae, ao,* and *au* from other vowels in a sequence. Hawaiian diphthongs are always stressed on the first vowel and are not as run-together as in English or Romance languages.

One of the biggest problems with Hawaiian words is figuring out where to put the stress. The basic rule is to accent the next to last syllable and alternating preceding syllables with the heaviest stress on the next to last. Thus Apapane is pronounced *AH-pah-PAH-nay*. An exception to this rule is that five-syllable words are stressed on the first and fourth. Unfortunately, in practice the rules of stress are difficult to apply because many words are compounds or have irregular accents. In proper Hawaiian orthography, irregular stress is indicated by a symbol called a macron, a horizontal bar over the stressed vowel. It is not exactly an irregular accent as in Spanish, but rather indicates a lengthening of the vowel sound. Some words have more than one macron, and the "normal" stress is also maintained secondarily. The absence of macrons and glottal stops in the English versions of Hawaiian words has led to many mispronunciations. Where necessary, proper pronunciation of some bird and place names is discussed herein.

For birders interested in learning the meanings of bird and place names, several Hawaiian dictionaries, from small pocket-size ones to huge library references, are available in bookstores throughout the islands. Two terms, however, must be defined here because they are used throughout this book to indicate directions. The usual compass directions are often not very useful on islands, but one is almost always aware of the location of the ocean and the mountains. *Makai* means "toward the sea" and *mauka* means "toward the mountain." These terms are very useful in Hawaii and are universally understood. You will hear them if you ask directions.

NAMES OF BIRDS

English names of birds used in this book are, for the most part, the same as those used in *A Field Guide to the Birds of Hawaii and the Tropical Pacific*. Those names in turn are based mostly on those of the 1983 AOU Check-list and subsequent supplements. The *Field Guide* names differed from AOU names in only 12 cases, and some of these have subsequently been changed by the AOU. Where use of a name would cause confusion, that alternative is given parenthetically. Because the original Hawaiian names of most native birds are now accepted as English names, they are written without macrons or glottal stops. As an aid to pronunciation, those that would be confusing are listed below in proper Hawaiian orthography with phonetic pronunciation.

nēnē	NAY-NAY
'ō'u	OH-OO
nuku-pu'u	NOO-koo-POO-oo
'akiapōlā'au	ah-KEE-ah-POE-LAH-OW
'alauahio	AH-low-ah-HEE-oh
'anianiau	AH-nee-ah-NEE-ow
'ākepa	AH-KEH-pah
'akeke'e	AH-keh-KAY-eh
'i'iwi	ee-EE-vee
'ākohekohe	AH-KOH-hay-KOH-hay
po'o-uli	POE-oh-OO-lee

List of Abbreviations

Av.	Avenue
Hwy.	Highway
NHP	National Historical Park
NHS	National Historic Site
NWR	National Wildlife Refuge
Res.	Reservoir
Rd.	Road
SP	State Park
St.	Street

INTRODUCTION

MEET HAWAII'S BIRDS

NATIVE FOREST BIRDS. The most distinctly Hawaiian of birds, and consequently the ones of greatest interest to visiting birders, are those that inhabit native forests. Although they belong to avian families found elsewhere in the world, all but one of the Hawaiian forest birds are *endemic* (i. e., found only in Hawaii). Species known in historic times included a hawk (Accipitridae), an owl (Strigidae), a crow (Corvidae), five species of honeyeater (Meliphagidae), a monarch flycatcher (Monarchidae), and members of two subfamilies of the large family Muscicapidae: an Old World warbler (Sylviinae) and five solitaires or thrushes (Turdinae). But by far the most distinctly Hawaiian element of the avifauna is a group of thirty species with highly varied adaptations known collectively as Hawaiian honeycreepers (**Figure 1**). The honeycreepers were long regarded as an endemic family, but now are usually classified as a subfamily (Drepanidinae) of the Fringillidae which also includes several kinds of mainland finches. Because not all of the honeycreepers actually feed on nectar, and because most of them are not superficially very finchlike, birders have given them the collective nickname "dreps," based on the subfamily name.

Surprisingly, these 45 species of forest birds are believed to have evolved from only eight or nine ancestral species. For this reason, the Hawaiian Islands are probably the world's premier natural laboratory of avian evolution, although the Galápagos are more famous in this regard. The process by which new species form is known as *speciation*. The Hawaiian solitaires (thrushes) illustrate how it works. The immediate ancestor of the 5 species was probably also the ancestor of Townsend's Solitaire of North America. The evidence for this relationship is found in similarities of both adult and juvenile plumages, bill shape, vocalizations, and nest construction as well as in the fact that Townsend's Solitaire (and probably its immediate ancestor) migrates long distances in small flocks. Thus it is an excellent candidate for an island colonizer. But the Hawaiian Islands are quite different ecologically from mainland North America, and the immigrant solitaires had to adapt to the local environment. Probably only one island was colonized initially (probably Kauai because the Kamao is the species most similar to mainland solitaires), but as the population built up, birds strayed to other islands that eventually all had solitaire populations.

Figure 1. Selected Hawaiian honeycreepers showing the range of bill variation. Painting by the author.

The separate island populations could then evolve independently. Among other changes, each island population developed its own vocal dialect, probably in much the same way that human languages change among isolated groups. That meant that if a solitaire from, say, Oahu happened to get to Kauai, it might not recognize the songs of the Kauai birds and in turn not be recognized by them. At that point, the two could be considered separate species because they would no longer interbreed. Because birds use song in territory defense, we can test this idea by playing tape recordings from one island to birds on another. If the song elicits no response, we can assume that the birds in question are different species. The Hawaiians noticed these song differences and gave the different populations, which correspond to the species recognized today, distinctive names. Somewhere along the line, one of the other populations reinvaded Kauai and became the ancestor of a second species there, the Puaiohi. The solitaires are a good example of speciation because they still all look more or less alike despite their bill shape and vocal differences; their interrelationship is obvious.

The Hawaiian honeycreepers, in contrast, have carried speciation to truly amazing extremes. Obviously, the group has inhabited the islands for a very long time. The founder species is believed to have been a bird similar to a goldfinch or siskin. But millions of years of speciation have led to an array of species many of which are not finchlike at all. Because so few birds have been able to colonize the islands, those that did found the field wide open. With so many "ecological niches" available by default, Hawaiian finches could evolve in directions unavailable to their mainland cousins. The group produced tanager-like fruit eaters (Ou), quasi-nuthatches (Akikiki), ersatz wood warblers (Maui Creeper), Rube Goldberg woodpeckers (Akiapolaau), honeyeater imitators (Akohekohe), egg-eating grosbeaks (Laysan Finch), miniature crossbills (Akepa), sickle-billed bark-pickers (Akialoa), nectar-feeders with both short (Apapane) and long (Iiwi) bills, and others with no close parallel anywhere (Maui Parrotbill, Poo-uli, Lanai Hookbill) in addition to fairly conventional finches (Palila). The derivation of many highly varied species from a single ancestor is called *adaptive radiation*, and the dreps are by far the best example among birds.

Sadly, Hawaii's forest bird legacy, from which so much remains to be learned, has been decimated and continues to lose ground. Of the 45 species, at least fifteen are extinct, some quite recently **(Figure 2)**. Of the remainder, over half are considered endangered or threatened. Some of these (e. g. Olomao, Bishop's Oo,

Figure 2. Ooaa, or Kauai Oo, photographed in 1975 in the Alakai Swamp, Kauai. Now extinct.

Nukupuu) are so rare that only a few living people have ever seen them. Others that were still "seeable" in the 1970s (e. g. Hawaiian Crow, Kamao, Puaiohi, Ou, Poo-uli) are now just as hard to find. The rest, however, can still be seen with a little effort, and a few are even abundant. Surviving native forest birds are, for the most part, restricted to montane habitats above 4,000 feet. Several factors contribute to this restriction,

Figure 3. Virgin Hawaiian rainforests, Alakai Swamp, Kauai.

but the most important is the presence of disease-carrying mosquitoes in the lowlands. Habitat destruction is also a factor, but native forest birds do not necessarily require native trees. Some of them do quite well in alien vegetation above 4,000 feet, but below that elevation even the few relatively pristine native plant communities lack the native birds once found in them. This elevational restriction helps to explain why native birds on Maui and Hawaii are doing better than those of Oahu or Molokai. Kauai reaches just over 4,000 ft., but because of its configuration it has more high-elevation habitat than the other lower islands. Above 4,000 feet, finding unspoiled habitat **(Figure 3)** becomes important. The rarer native birds tend to be those that are so specialized that they can tolerate little habitat disturbance. Pristine habitats are today disappearing even far from roads and other obvious disturbances. One of the most insidious threats is posed by feral pigs, which go through the forest like living bulldozers, rooting up the understory plants and leaving pools where mosquitoes can breed. Today's pigs are much bigger than those brought in by the original Hawaiians (over the years, pig hunters have purposely "bred up" the stock by releasing big European hogs to the wild) and far more destructive. They are inexorably penetrating further and further into the native forests. The drastic decline in the population of the Poo-uli during the past decade can be attributed almost entirely to habitat destruction by feral pigs.

NATIVE WATER BIRDS. Hawaii's native water birds **(Figure 4)** are less distinctive than the forest birds, but nevertheless include several endemic species. The most famous is the Nene or Hawaiian Goose which nearly went extinct earlier this century but was saved at the eleventh hour by a captive breeding and reintroduction program. It is the State Bird of Hawaii (as far as the state is concerned, its name is Nene, not Hawaiian Goose, the AOU Check-list notwithstanding). Included here because of its obvious relationship, the Nene is not really a wetland bird. It has adapted to life in dry grasslands and lava flows far from water. Hawaii also has 2 endemic ducks related to the Mallard, the Koloa (Hawaiian Duck) on the main islands, and the Laysan Duck isolated on remote Laysan. These have recently been joined by the Fulvous Whistling-

Figure 4. Hawaiian Native Waterbirds: a) Black-crowned Night-Heron, adult; b) Black-crowned Night-Heron, juvenile; c) Koloa, or Hawaiian Duck, drake; d) Koloa hen; e) Nene, or Hawaiian Goose; f) Common Moorhen, Hawaiian subspecies; g) Hawaiian Coot; h) Black-necked Stilt.

Duck (possibly introduced), a species found nearly worldwide. Another recent arrival is the Pied-billed Grebe from North America. Considering the rarity of successful island colonizations, the fact that these two have happened in the same decade and have been witnessed by scientists is remarkable indeed. The only indigenous heron in the islands is the Black-crowned Night-Heron, another nearly cosmopolitan species. It does not differ, even subspecifically, from members of the species in California. The rail family (Rallidae) is today represented by a local subspecies of Common Moorhen and by the Hawaiian Coot, sometimes regarded as a subspecies of American Coot. Two small rails that survived into historic times are extinct. The only shorebird to breed in Hawaii is the local subspecies of Black-necked Stilt.

Hawaiian water birds have fared little better than the forest birds, but the threats to them are different. The most obvious problem is the destruction of wetland habitats. Ponds and marshes have the unfortunate characteristic of being found along the coast on land that can easily be used for human residences, resort hotels, and golf courses. Waikiki was once a huge wetland; the canal called Ala Wai was built to drain it. Virtually all of Hawaii's natural wetland habitats have succumbed to such pressure, and the water birds have had to settle for artificial wetlands such as fishponds, taro patches, and sugar mill settling basins. But habitat is only one of the problems faced by wetland birds. All of them nest on the ground and are vulnerable to such introduced predators as dogs, cats, and especially mongooses. The fact that the Koloa survived naturally only on Kauai is probably attributable to the absence of the mongoose there. Several national wildlife refuges and a few state reserves have been established to provide secure nesting habitat for wetland birds. Although all native water birds are considered endangered, the birder can easily see them in these protected areas.

BREEDING SEABIRDS. Because of their strategic mid-ocean location and their lack of ground predators, the Hawaiian Islands were ideal nesting grounds for many seabirds that roam the world's oceans. Before the coming of man, seabirds bred throughout the archipelago but now only a few breed successfully on the larger islands. Fortunately, numerous offshore islets still provide nesting sites. All such small islands are state wildlife sanctuaries and landing on them is illegal without a permit. Fortunately for the birder, several such islands are close enough to shore that one can observe the nesting birds without disturbance. The Northwestern Hawaiian Islands form one of the world's most important seabird nurseries (Figure 5). Most of these islands are uninhabited and included in the

Figure 5. Mixed seabird nesting colony, Eastern I., Midway.

Hawaiian Islands National Wildlife Refuge, established by President Theodore Roosevelt in 1906. Two Hawaiian seabirds, the Bonin Petrel and Tristram's Storm-Petrel, nest nowhere else in the archipelago. That is almost true of the Black-footed Albatross and Blue-gray Noddy, both of which nest elsewhere only on islands off Niihau. Some of the seabirds that breed in the Hawaiian Islands are present all year, but others disperse widely once the chicks fledge **(Figure 6)**.

Among the main Hawaiian Islands, the nesting seabirds include an albatross, two petrels, three shearwaters, a storm-petrel, two tropicbirds, three boobies, one frigatebird, and five terns. Most of them nest on offshore islets, but the Hawaiian (Dark-rumped) Petrel, Townsend's (Newell's) Shearwater, and probably the Band-rumped Storm-Petrel nest high in the mountains. The only others that are able to nest on the main islands are the Red-footed Booby (because it nests in trees and mongooses rarely climb), a few Wedge-tailed Shearwaters (although with little success because of predation), and Black Noddies (which nest in shear sea cliffs). Several seabirds are so common in Hawaiian waters that they could be called "hard to miss." The birder should become thoroughly familiar with Red-footed Booby, Wedge-tailed Shearwater, Great Frigatebird, and both noddies so that less common species will be instantly noticed.

THE VISITORS. Many familiar, and a great many unfamiliar, birds in the Hawaiian Islands are seasonal visitors or occasional wanderers **(Figure 6)**. For the resident birder familiar with Hawaiian birds, it is these visitors that provide most of the birding excitement. Almost any bird that migrates long distances could show up in Hawaii, but the regular visitors fall into a few well-defined groupings as described below.

Pelagic seabirds. Numerous species of ocean wanderers have been recorded from Hawaiian waters. These birds tend to stay in deep water far from continental shores, but because the islands are the tops of oceanic mountains with no surrounding shallow shelf, pelagic birds approach more closely. They are unlikely to be seen in the shallow channels that separate Molokai, Maui, Lanai, and Kahoolawe (those islands were united as one, called Maui Nui, during the last glaciation about 12,000 years ago and the channels represent the flooded lowlands of that island), but the deeper channels between Kauai and Oahu and between Oahu and Molokai can be productive for migratory seabirds in spring and fall. Another good place to look is off the Kona Coast of the Big Island where very deep water is present right offshore. Because so few birders have looked for seabirds around Hawaii, the species composition of this pelagic avifauna is not well known; new and exciting discoveries are being made all the time. Species that are known to pass through Hawaiian waters in numbers include Sooty Shearwater, Mottled Petrel, Black-winged Petrel, Leach's Storm-Petrel, Red Phalarope, and Arctic Tern.

Gulls and terns. Among human visitors, one of the most frequently asked questions is why there are no gulls in Hawaii. The impression is fairly accurate despite the presence of a few stray gulls every winter. Mainland harbors echo with the calls of gulls, whereas those in Hawaii are silent. Gulls avoid Hawaii for several reasons. Worldwide, gulls are mostly birds of cold seas or inland waters and are replaced in the

FIGURE 6.
SEASONAL OCCURRENCE CHART OF MIGRATORY BIRDS IN THE HAWAIIAN ISLANDS

Code

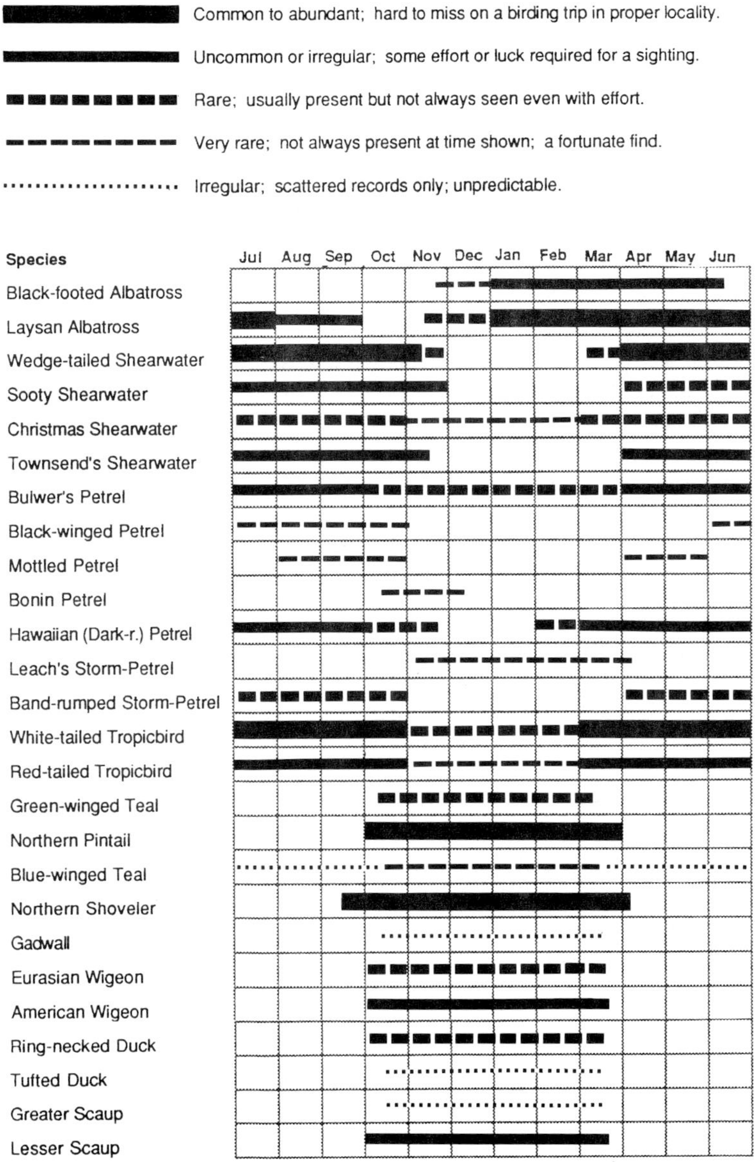

Common to abundant; hard to miss on a birding trip in proper locality.
Uncommon or irregular; some effort or luck required for a sighting.
Rare; usually present but not always seen even with effort.
Very rare; not always present at time shown; a fortunate find.
Irregular; scattered records only; unpredictable.
Species
Jul
Aug
Sep
Oct
Nov
Dec
Jan
Feb
Mar
Apr
May
Jun
Black-footed Albatross
Laysan Albatross
Wedge-tailed Shearwater
Sooty Shearwater
Christmas Shearwater
Townsend's Shearwater
Bulwer's Petrel
Black-winged Petrel
Mottled Petrel
Bonin Petrel
Hawaiian (Dark-r.) Petrel
Leach's Storm-Petrel
Band-rumped Storm-Petrel
White-tailed Tropicbird
Red-tailed Tropicbird
Green-winged Teal
Northern Pintail
Blue-winged Teal
Northern Shoveler
Gadwall
Eurasian Wigeon
American Wigeon
Ring-necked Duck
Tufted Duck
Greater Scaup
Lesser Scaup

Figure 6 (cont'd)

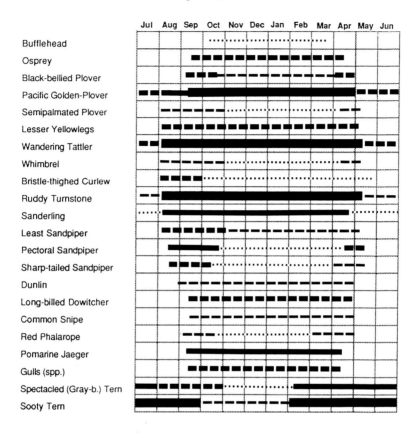

tropics by boobies, tropicbirds, and terns. Hawaiian waters are too warm for them. Also, most gulls are adapted to feed in the shallows over the continental shelf. Many of the gulls that manage to reach the islands eventually starve to death. An impressive number of gull species have been recorded, the most frequent being Ring-billed **(Figure 7)**, Laughing, and Bonaparte's. A few terns usually associated with the mainland also show up from time to time, and the Pomarine Jaeger is a regular winter visitor in fair numbers. The best places to look for stray gulls and terns are wetland habitats near the coast.

Shorebirds. Several migratory shorebirds **(Figure 8)** are among Hawaii's most familiar birds, and have even been immortalized in Hawaiian songs. (Ask a Hawaiian band to play *Ulili E*; they will be impressed that you know about it and you will hear a wonderful tune with vocals that imitate the Wandering Tattler's call.) The Pacific Golden-Plover is so familiar to people in the islands that most are surprised to learn that it does not nest here. Others that can be found in any shoreline or wetland habitat include Ruddy Turnstone, Sanderling, and Wandering Tattler. Others, such as Black-

Figure 7. Ring-billed Gull, the most frequently seen gull in the Hawaiian Islands.

bellied Plover, Common Snipe, and Lesser Yellowlegs are rare but present nearly every winter in low numbers. Many shorebirds do not remain long in the main Hawaiian Islands but use them as a stopover during spring and fall migrations. Species that pass through every year include Bristle-thighed Curlew, Sharp-tailed Sandpiper, Pectoral Sandpiper, and Least Sandpiper. Because of the islands' central location, the rarer shorebirds comprise an interesting mix of New World and Old World species. Because shorebird habitat is limited in the islands, the birds tend to concentrate in a few "hot spots." Most of these are covered later in the Site Guide.

Waterfowl. Many ducks **(Figure 9)** and a few geese winter in the Hawaiian Islands. The vast majority of all wintering waterfowl belong to just two species, Northern Shoveler and Northern Pintail. A second group of species are much less numerous but present every year. This group includes American Wigeon, Green-winged Teal, and Lesser Scaup. As with the shorebirds, ducks in Hawaii include a blend of New and Old World species. Although not present every year, Eurasian Wigeon, Garganey, and Tufted Duck show up with some regularity. Five species of migratory geese have been found in Hawaii, but the only one that is at all regular is the Canada Goose. Wintering waterfowl in Hawaii are almost always seen on ponds and reservoirs rather than on the ocean.

Birds of prey. Only a few migratory birds of prey have been recorded in Hawaii and most of them are known from one or two records. The only species to be recorded annually is the Osprey. In recent years, the Peregrine Falcon has turned up with increasing frequency, and there have been several recent sightings of Northern Harriers, once considered strictly accidental.

Introduced Birds . The first bird brought to Hawaii by man was the Red Junglefowl **(Figure 10)** which arrived with the first Polynesians. The first European visitors brought a second one, the Wild Turkey. Since then, the islands have seen a steady stream of new avian immigrants. Hawaii has become notorious among birders as the place with more introduced birds than anywhere else. Their consternation is understandable because when most birders think of introduced birds, they envision urban "weed" species that present little challenge and even less interest. To be sure, Hawaii has its share of such species. However, many of its introduced birds **(Figure 11)** seem almost like native birds. They have repopulated lowland forests that are now uninhabitable for native species. We can sympathize with the Hawaii residents

Figure 8. Representative migratory shorebirds of Hawaii: a) Pacific Golden-Plover, male in spring; b) Pacific Golden- Plover, non-breeding plumage most often seen in the islands; c) Semipalmated Plover; d) Least Sandpiper; e) Ruddy Turnstone, nonbreeding plumage; f) Ruddy Turnstone, breeding plumage; g) Sanderling; h) Wandering Tattler.

Figure 9. Migratory ducks of the Hawaiian Islands; a) Northern Pintail hen; b) Northern Pintail drake; c) Northern Shoveler ; d) Mallards; e) Green-winged Teal; f) Blue-winged Teal; g) Lesser Scaup; h) Ring-necked Duck.

11

who, finding themselves in a nearly birdless world, organized the Hui Manu, a private society that from the 1920s to the 1950s took as its mission the introduction of birds from all over the world. Recent studies have shown that, with a few exceptions, the successful aliens do not compete with native species but rather fill unoccupied niches in the environment. Indeed, alien birds are far outnumbered by native species in forest habitats above 4,000 feet.

Figure 10. Red Junglefowl, Hawaii's first introduced bird.

Introduced birds that are regularly found in such forests include Northern Cardinal, Red-billed Leiothrix, Hwa-mei (Melodious Laughing-thrush), and the ubiquitous Japanese White-eye. Considering that about fifty alien species are established in Hawaii, that so few have invaded native habitats is remarkable. In the Hawaiian lowlands, virtually the entire avifauna, like the human population, is made up of immigrants. Hawaii's introduced birds are not without their redeeming virtues. The interactions of the members of this artificial avifauna have provided scientists with insights into the process of island colonization and avian community dynamics. Also, the introduced bird community provides much enjoyment and enlightenment for people who otherwise might rarely see birds at all.

Most species introduced to Hawaii were brought in because they were considered attractive in some way. Many of them were obtained through the cage-bird trade and represent species familiar to pet-store visitors. But among these rather uninteresting birds are some surprising ones. The last species introduced by the Hui Manu was the Island Swiftlet, which is now an endangered species on its home island of Guam. Other unusual introductions include Cattle Egret, Barn Owl, Eurasian Skylark, Greater Necklaced Laughing-thrush, and Western Meadowlark. Introduction of alien species became illegal in the early 1960s, but the two bulbuls were brought in surreptitiously after that date. All alien species currently considered established in Hawaii have been in the islands for at least a quarter century.

In addition to the birds brought in for ornamental or sentimental reasons are a number of species introduced mainly to give hunters something to shoot. The Pittman-Robertson Act set up a fund earmarked for the benefit of game species. Because Hawaii had no huntable upland birds, it used its share of Pittman-Robertson funds to introduce some. At one point, the state was even involved in the ridiculous activity of destroying native habitats to "improve" them for introduced game birds! Happily, that mentality no longer holds sway. As with the ornamental birds and songbirds, the game birds include some surprising species. Along with the expected francolins, **(Figure 12)**

Figure 11. A selection of birds introduced to Hawaii: a) Spotted Dove; b) Zebra Dove; c) Common Myna; d) Red-crested Cardinal; e) Japanese White-eye; f) White-rumped Shama; g) Red-vented Bulbul; h) Red-whiskered Bulbul.

13

quails, and pheasants are Chestnut-bellied Sandgrouse and Mourning Dove.

HABITATS FOR BIRDS IN HAWAII

URBAN HABITATS. The first birds a visitor is likely to see in Hawaii are those adapted to life in proximity to human activities. Some species seem to be just as happy perching on concrete as on trees. Others, while found in urban areas **(Figure 13)**, are restricted to green islands such as parks and tree-shaded lawns. Most urban birds are introduced species, but at least two natives, Pacific Golden-Plover and Common Fairy-Tern, can be found in Honolulu parks. Kapiolani Park in Waikiki is probably the most productive urban birding locality in terms of number of species. Most of the trees and shrubs found in Hawaiian urban habitats are widespread tropical ornamentals; very few are indigenous to the islands.

PASTURES, FIELDS, AND OTHER GRASSLANDS. Grassland habitats in Hawaii are almost all artificial. Huge tracts of what was once native forest today are man-made grasslands **(Figure 14)**, maintained in that state by cattle grazing. No native birds are restricted to grasslands, and only the Short-eared Owl is found in them regularly. Pastures are excellent habitat for many of the introduced game birds such as Common Pheasants and Wild Turkeys, and the Japanese Quail seems to be

Figure 12. *Gray Francolin*

Figure 13. *Urban habitat; view into Manoa Valley from Waikiki, Oahu.*

Figure 14. *Man-made grassland habitat along Saddle Road, Hawaii.*

found only in fallow fields. A few introduced songbirds including Eurasian Skylark and Western Meadowlark favor pastures. Other species, particularly the waxbills and mannikins, prefer taller ungrazed grasses and are thus found in weedy places such as borders of cane fields and golf courses rather than in close-cropped fields. Grassland habitats are very extensive on all the islands, but the largest expanses are on Hawaii and Maui. The main pasture grasses are aliens from Africa and North America. Several ornamental grasses have escaped from gardens and become pests. Fountain grass, the clumpy white-plumed grass that blankets the lava flows of North Kona and South Kohala on the Big Island, is a particularly noxious weed despite its attractiveness. It is unpalatable to cattle and a major fire hazard. The alien grasses provide food for weed birds such as Red Avadavat, Warbling Silverbill, and several waxbills.

WETLANDS. As indicated earlier, wetlands in modern Hawaii are virtually all artificial. The islands' natural marshes and ponds have long since been drained for agriculture or urbanization. Man-made wetlands are, however, acceptable to native water birds. Some of the best wetland habitat today is created by farming operations (**Figure 15**) that raise such things as freshwater prawns and taro (the starchy root usually made into poi, a local delicacy). The lowlands of all islands are dotted with small reservoirs used in the irrigation of sugar cane. Such reservoirs are generally rather sterile, probably because of frequent water fluctuations. Nevertheless, if time is not a factor, it is a good idea to check all such ponds that are accessible. As an example of what can be found, a Red-necked Grebe, Hawaii's first, was found by a mainland birder on Halenananu Reservoir on Kauai in 1988. Normally, this pond has nothing more than a few Hawaiian Coots, so local birders usually pass it by. Settling basins are a little more predictable although they, too, tend to vary from year to year in their birding productivity. A good settling basin at just the right stage can be a great place for shorebirds, especially peeps. More reliable are the managed wetlands of the national wildlife refuges.

NATIVE RAINFOREST. Hawaiian rainforests, although they qualify for the title on the basis of rainfall, are not very similar to tropical rainforests on the continents. They differ in being dominated by only a few tree species, the most important of which are the red-flowered ohia-lehua (usually just called ohia), a member of the eucalyptus family (Myrtaceae), and koa, a type of acacia (Fabaceae). Ohia is an amazingly adaptable species with a bewildering variety of growth forms. It is not only a pioneer tree on fresh lava flows, but forms the canopy of mature forests. Although an individual

Figure 15. Taro farming creates freshwater wetlands, Hanalei National Wildlife Refuge, Kauai.

tree may be seasonal, some ohia trees are always in bloom. The red shaving-brush flowers **(Figure 16)** produce copious amounts of nectar, and a tree in heavy bloom is a bird magnet (not just for nectar-feeders because insects also are attracted to the flowers). In very wet areas **(Figure 17)**, the entire forest canopy may be ohia, usually with a continuous understory of hapuu (tree fern). In areas that are not so wet, koa trees become intermingled and often are emergent over the ohia canopy. Such trees provide nest sites for Hawaiian Hawks. In forests with less rainfall still, koa may predominate or more often share the canopy with ohia. The mixed koa-ohia forests **(Figure 18)** tend

Figure 16. Red flowers of the ohia-lehua tree, an important source of nectar for native forest birds.

Figure 17. Tree-fern understory in wet ohia forest, Kilauea Forest Reserve, Hawaii.

Figure 18. Mixed koa/ohia forest on slope of Mauna Loa (Mauna Kea in background), Kulani Tract, Hawaii.

to be at higher elevations than wet forests, especially on the Big Island, and are the richest habitat for native birds today.

Because of its propensity to pioneer on lava flows **(Figure 19)**, ohia sometimes grows in dense stands of nearly uniform age. Such plantationlike forests go through what is now believed to be a natural cycle called die-back, wherein virtually all the canopy trees die at about the same time allowing new ohia trees to sprout beneath them. In a pristine environment, the die-back cycle was not detrimental to birds because there were always areas of mature forest available when one area died back. Now, however, ohia forests are much less extensive and there are fewer "escape routes" for birds in a die-back area. Also, alien weeds such as blackberry and banana poka (a type of passion fruit) can now invade die-back areas before new ohia trees can grow, thus breaking the cycle. Birders will notice large tracts of forest in various stages of die-back along the Saddle Road above Hilo, Stainback Highway, and in Volcano Village. Whether these

Figure 19. Ohia saplings pioneering on recent lava, Hawaii Volcanoes National Park.

areas will be able to withstand the encroachment of weeds and return to native forest is an open question.

MAMANE-NAIO FOREST. A distinctive forest type found in dry (but not desertlike) areas usually at high elevations, this habitat is dominated by its namesake trees, mamane (a legume) and naio (a member of the Myoporaceae, a mostly Australian family). Both trees are shrubby and form no closed canopy, so these forests are open and parklike with a grassy understory **(Figure 20)**. The most important belt of mamane-naio forest encircles Mauna Kea above 6,000 ft. It is the only place where the Palila, a finchlike Hawaiian honeycreeper, still lives. Several other dreps, including the rare Akiapolaau, are found here as well, especially when the yellow-flowered mamane is in bloom.

LOWLAND DRY FOREST. In pre-human times, this habitat was one of the most important for native birds. Now, it is reduced to pitiful remnants inhabited mainly by alien species. One of these remnants **(Figure 21)** is near Puu Waa Waa on Hawaii. Here, one can still find such native dry-forest trees as naio (described above), lama (a native persimmon), halapepe (a relative of Dracaena), and wiliwili (a native coralbean).

Figure 20. Mamane/naio forest near Puu Ahumoa, Hawaii.

Figure 21. Relict lowland dry forest, Puu Waa Waa Ranch, Hawaii.

Nowadays, almost equally common in such dry forests are introduced trees such as silk oak from Australia and jacaranda from tropical America. The only native birds still found in this forest are Common Amakihi, Hawaiian Hawk, and Short-eared Owl. Introduced birds, however, have found this to be a rich habitat and Saffron Finches, Yellow-fronted Canaries, waxbills, mannikins, and numerous game birds abound.

Since the mid-1800s, a new type of lowland dry forest has become widespread in coastal and dry upland areas on all the islands. Groves of algoroba, a kind of mesquite from Central America known locally as kiawe (*kee-AH-veh*), are now characteristic of dry habitats in Hawaii such as those along the northern Kona Coast of the Big Island and the Kihei area of Maui. Kiawe thickets **(Figure 22)** harbor no native birds, but many introduced ones such as Yellow-billed Cardinals, Gray Francolins, and Warbling Silverbills thrive in them. In some areas, scattered kiawe tree with grassy ground cover produce a habitat that mimics the African savannah. Other dry lowland areas have become nearly a monoculture of haole koa (*koa-haole* in Hawaiian), another weedy neotropical legume. Haole koa thickets are of little interest to the birder, but on Oahu, at least, often harbor Japanese Bush-warblers.

Figure 22. Kiawe scrub, South Kohala District, Hawaii.

INTRODUCED WET FORESTS. The lush forests in the mountains behind Honolulu, with their dense foliage, vine-draped understory, and multiple-layered growth form seem perfectly natural **(Figure 23)**. The fact is that these hills were nearly denuded of trees earlier in the 20th century and these forests are composed almost entirely of alien trees and shrubs. They are the descendants of a forest type found throughout the tropical Pacific in association with man. Elsewhere, it is known as agricultural forest because the trees are mostly plants useful for food, fiber, or medicines. The name is a little misleading because it implies more human management than such forests normally receive. Even in Hawaii, such plants as mango, mountain apple, kukui (candlenut), breadfruit, lilikoi (passionfruit), and guava predominate. At higher elevations, these exotic forests mingle with the native rainforests. These forests can provide a lot of frustration for the novice mainland birder in Hawaii. One can waste a lot of time stopping in seemingly auspicious-looking habitat only to find the same species that were common in Kapiolani Park. You have to learn to resist the urge to stop in every wooded area. The one exception to this caveat is Kauai, where one has to search such lowland forests to find the Greater Necklaced Laughing-thrush.

Figure 23. An artificial rainforest of alien trees, Lyon Arboretum, Oahu.

19

BARREN AND ALPINE HABITATS. Hawaii's four highest peaks, Mauna Kea, Mauna Loa, Haleakala, and Hualalai, all have alpine zones (Figure 24) at their summits. Tree line at this latitude is about 7,000 feet in most places. Surprisingly, a few birds are able to use these rocky and seemingly sterile areas. The Hawaiian (Dark-rumped) Petrel nests in burrows on these mountaintops, and on Hawaii a population of the Omao, usually a rainforest species, lives above tree line on Mauna Loa. Chukars are fairly common in the alpine zone of Haleakala. On the Big Island, barren areas are found at all elevations as a result of volcanic eruptions. The Nene has adapted to life among the lava flows, which afford it a modicum of protection from predators.

Figure 24. Barren alpine zone, Haleakala National Park, Maui.

BIRDING IN THE ALOHA STATE

Birding on tropical islands is different in several respects from birding on the mainland. Not only are you presented with an unfamiliar avifauna, but a number of possibly unanticipated logistical problems present themselves. This section will give you some tips that will make your Hawaiian birding experience more enjoyable. The most important recommendation, that applies to all aspects of birding in a new area, is "Do your homework." Reading this guide before you leave home will save a lot of time in the field, as will spending a little time looking over maps so you will not be totally bewildered when you arrive. Many birders tend to overlook the "front matter" of their field guides and other references, but often some of the most fundamental and important things one needs to know are contained therein. Don't skip the introductions.

Climate and weather. Hawaii is justly famous for its wonderful year-round climate, warm with cooling tradewinds. The islands lie outside the usual paths of Pacific hurricanes and such major storms are infrequent. However, like anywhere else, Hawaii sometimes has bad weather. The weather in Waikiki, which lies in the "rain shadow" of the Koolau Mountains, is not really typical. Tourist developments throughout the islands obviously are built in places that, in their natural state, would be arid. The lush greenery you see around hotels is the result of careful irrigation. Common sense will tell you that the lush forests in the mountains have to receive frequent rain. Also for obvious reasons, relatively undisturbed native forests (where the rare native birds are found) tend to be in the rainiest places. Sturdy rain gear is essential. If you wear glasses, you will want a hat with a brim. The "good" forests also are at fairly high elevations. Do not naively assume, as some have to their regret, that because Hawaii is tropical you can just get wet and not be uncomfortable (or even become dangerously chilled).

Weather in Hawaii is fairly predictable in a broad sense, but can change drastically from day to day. Much of the variation depends on the strength of the northeast tradewinds. The stronger the trades, the more rain will fall. As these moisture-laden winds strike the windward (eastern) side of an island, they are forced upward by the mountains and cooled, causing condensation and rainfall on the slopes. On Maui and Hawaii, where the mountains are massive, most of the rain may fall on the windward slope. On Kauai, Oahu, and Molokai the mountains are not so high and much of the rain spills over to the leeward slope. Rain clouds hang almost continuously over the mountains behind Honolulu, but only occasionally invade the lowlands. It is this dry coast-wet mountains regime that produces Hawaii's fabled rainbows **(Figure 25)**. A characteristic weather forecast for Honolulu is "sunny at the beach with mauka showers." The leeward sides of all major mountains are dry because the mountains cast a "rain shadow." Sometimes, however, this fairly predictable island-generated weather pattern is interrupted by fronts that override local topographic effects. Occasionally the northeast trades cease and warm humid air moves in from the southwest. These periods of "kona weather" can be hot, muggy, and very uncomfortable. Fortunately, they do not usually last more than a week or two. Kona weather can happen any time of year. Contrary to popular notions, Hawaii does experience noticeable seasonal change. The warmest weather is usually in August and September, the coolest from January to March. The "rainy season" begins in late November and extends through mid-March. Areas such as the Hamakua Coast of the Big Island that tend to be rainy year-round can have downpours for weeks on end during this season.

Hawaii's usually crystal blue skies are occasionally sullied by volcanic activity. During eruptions on the Big Island, volcanic smog or "vog" sometimes reaches as far as Honolulu, especially during kona weather. At such times, haze may obscure normally

Figure 25. Rainbow over Waimea Canyon, Kauai.

clear vistas. Fortunately Hawaii's volcanoes are "clean" in that they do not produce dust or ash. However, the sulphurous fumes produce natural acid rain downwind and can be dangerous to persons with respiratory problems. In any case, if you are fortunate enough to be on the Big Island during an eruption, the haze is a small price to pay for witnessing one of nature's most awe-inspiring phenomena **(Figure 26)**.

Figure 26. Active pahoehoe lava flow, October 1989, Kalapana, Hawaii.

Equipment. Basic birding equipment is the same for Hawaii as elsewhere, but local conditions can make some differences in your choice of such things as binoculars. Hawaiian forests are often rainy and dark, but birds can often be approached closely. Binoculars with good light-gathering and close-focusing capabilities are an advantage. A good spotting scope is essential for observing birds on distant mudflats and offshore islands. Your Hawaiian birding will be greatly enhanced if you have one. Many of the birding sites described in this book require some hiking to get to the good birds. Hiking in Hawaiian forests is difficult at best. Most trails are not well graded and mud is an ever-present fact of life. Obviously, you will need good footwear, but there are several different ways to deal with the problems. Some people never like wet feet. For them, waterproof boots are recommended. Many hikers find such boots uncomfortable and prefer standard leather ones instead. They have the advantage over most rubber boots of giving better traction and ankle support, but no matter how much waterproofing you use, you will eventually have wet feet if you wear leather boots. Fortunately, the air temperature is never severely cold in the rainforest, so wet feet may be a necessary evil. Many local residents prefer to hike in tabis, socklike things with a heavy felt sole sewn in. These were originally designed for reef-walking, and protect only the bottoms of the feet. They are available from fishermen's supply stores in Honolulu. With tabis, you simply decide to get your feet wet and forget about it. Their disadvantage is that they provide no support whatever, but if you are used to going barefoot, tabis may be for you. They certainly are easier to clean than boots.

Obviously, a local field guide is essential. This book tells you where to find birds, not how to identify them. You will need either the small photographically illustrated *Hawaii's Birds,* the larger and more detailed *A Field Guide to the Birds of Hawaii and the Tropical Pacific,* or both. These and other supplemental guides are listed in For Further Information. Good maps are also a necessity. Space does not permit the inclusion of large-scale maps herein, but several excellent ones are available at convenience stores everywhere in Hawaii. Among the best are those in the James A. Bier series, mostly published by the University of Hawaii Press. For the traveler, these maps are superior to those in the *Atlas of Hawaii* (also University of Hawaii Press), although the *Atlas* is an excellent home reference.

Interisland travel. The Hawaiian Islands are very well served by airlines. Interisland flights are frequent and prices reasonable on the major carriers. They usually will honor each other's tickets, so you can keep your schedule flexible. Most visitors are surprised to learn that there is essentially no surface transportation for passengers between islands. That is particularly unfortunate for birders, because it removes one potential means of seeing pelagic birds. Several cruise ships ply the interisland waters, but they mostly travel at night and spend the day in port. They are by no means to be considered basic transportation. One cruise route that has some potential for birding leaves Honolulu in the evening and travels to Kauai, circling the leeward side of the island during the day before putting into Nawiliwili Harbor. These are good waters for seabirds and largely unbirded.

Because so many people travel between islands, rental cars are everywhere available in abundance. With so much competition, bargain prices can often be found if you shop around. Locally owned agencies tend to be cheaper than the national chains, but not always. Most companies offer a variety of vehicles, but four-wheel-drives are scarce. On Kauai, the only such vehicles for rent are small open jeeps that are not very serviceable for driving through mud. On Hawaii, good 4WD vehicles are available from Harper's Car and Truck Rentals (808/969-1478) in Hilo. You will probably want a four-wheel-drive if you plan to bird the Saddle Road sites discussed in this book. If you rent a car on the Big Island, all rental agencies (including Harper's who regularly rent to hunters who virtually have to drive on the Saddle Road) will tell you that Route 200 is off limits. (Some agencies used to say driving the Saddle Road was illegal, which it was not.) You may even be given a map that shows the Saddle Road as a dotted line and carries a warning that the road is unpaved and dangerous. These warnings, quite frankly, are lies and have been for at least two decades. The road, which is the key to seeing birds on the Big Island, is paved throughout its length and most of it is as good as any road on the island. The "bad" spots are currently being improved. I do not understand the reason for the restriction other than mindless clinging to outdated rules and the fact that there are no services on the Saddle Road. Probably the rental agencies just do not want to be bothered with rescuing you if you get into trouble "way up there." In any case, do not mention your intention to drive on the Saddle Road to the rental agent or you may not get a car. The only real effect of the contract restrictions is that if you purchase optional insurance coverage when you rent a vehicle, it will not cover you on the Saddle Road. You will be driving "at your own risk." However, if you have auto insurance at home it probably covers you in a rental car as well, and several credit cards offer automatic insurance coverage that is unaffected by local restrictions. Also, if you do have a breakdown or an accident, you will have to arrange for towing yourself rather than calling your rental company. These comments apply to driving on unpaved roads on all islands, so check your insurance before you rent if you think you may want to get off the paved highway (as birders often do).

Birding tours and excursions. One of the best ways for a mainlander to see a lot of Hawaiian birds in a short time is to join an organized tour **(Figure 27)**. Most of the major birding tour companies offer occasional Hawaii trips. Voyagers International offers tours led by the author at least once a year. Be sure when selecting a tour that you choose one with an experienced leader who has access to restricted areas. Permits to visit many wildlife refuges and preserves require a fairly lengthy application process, and most one-time tours will not have made the effort. Many Hawaii natural history tours, including some of those led by the author, are fairly general in their approach and, although you will see a good representation of Hawaiian birds on one of these, are not intended for the dedicated birder intent on seeing as many species as possible. If you fall into the latter category, be sure the tour you select is promoted as primarily a birding tour. On a good two-week birding tour in spring or fall, you can expect to see around a hundred species. The record (108 species) for such a tour with a large (16 persons) group was set by an American Birding Association party sponsored by Voyagers International and led by the author in April 1989. In October-November the same year, with a group of six and a great deal of luck, the author set the all-time two-week (actually 15 days) record at 120 species. I doubt this total will be equalled or exceeded any time soon.

Figure 27. American Birding Association 1990 tour group led by the author (in red cap), Kulani Tract, Hawaii.

The Hawaii Audubon Society sponsors shorter field trips several times a year and occasional longer ones. News of these trips is published monthly in the society's journal *'Elepaio*. The Nature Conservancy of Hawaii sponsors hikes, usually with a nominal fee, periodically into their preserves **(Figure 28)**. The Audubon Society trips are mostly for birding, but the Nature Conservancy ones are more habitat-oriented and may or may not get you to the best spots for avian rarities. If you are interested only in birds, be sure to inquire ahead as to exactly where a given hike will go and whether the group will be looking mainly for birds or concentrating on other rare Hawaiian animals and plants. In either case, the hikes are well worth taking.

Figure 28. Entrance sign to the Nature Conservancy of Hawaii's Waikamol Preserve, Maui.

A few local tour operators, as well as the author, are available for private hire. Two that can provide competent birding assistance are Mark Collins of Hawaiian Sunrise Excursions and International Expeditions, Inc., and David Kuhn of Terran Tours. These and other Hawaii tour operators are listed below:

Hawaii Audubon Society
212 Merchant St., Rm. 320
P. O. Box 22832
Honolulu HI 96813
(808) 528-1432

David Kuhn
Terran Tours
P. O. Box 1018
Waimea, HI 96796
(808) 335-3313

Nature Conservancy of Hawaii
1116 Smith St.
Honolulu HI 96817
(808) 537-4508

H. Douglas Pratt
4583 Downing Drive
Baton Rouge LA 70809
(504) 928-4297

Voyagers International
P. O. Box 915
Ithaca NY 14851
(800) 633-0299

Oahu

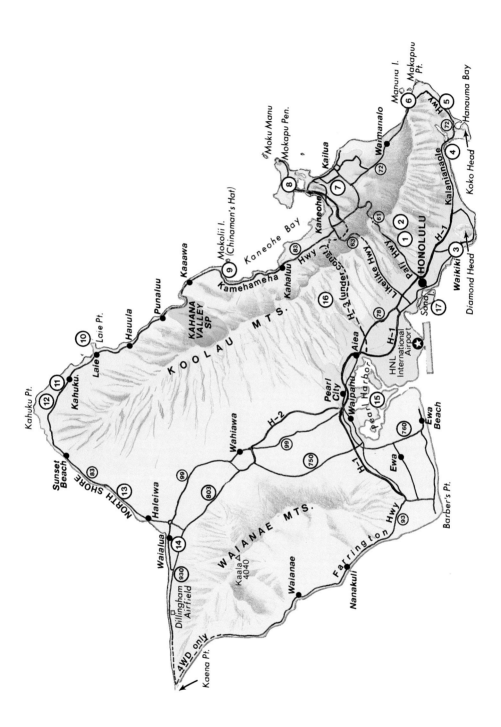

OAHU

Although only the third in size among the main Hawaiian Islands, Oahu is truly the heart of Hawaii. The City and County of Honolulu, a single entity that includes the whole island, is home to about eighty percent of the state's population of a little over a million. The political and cultural center of the State of Hawaii, Honolulu is a major city even in the national context. Although it has many of the same urban problems as other large urban areas, such as frustrating traffic congestion, it is generally a very pleasant city for the birder. It has no neighborhoods that would be considered slums by mainland standards, has numerous parks and other open areas, and is generally clean and modern. Waikiki, an enclave separated from the main part of Honolulu by a canal called the Ala Wai (it means "water way," so saying "Ala Wai Canal" is like saying "Rio Grande River"), is a major tourist mecca where nearly all the hotels on Oahu are located.

Oahu is dominated by two parallel mountain ranges, the Waianaes in the west and the Koolaus in the east. A broad valley devoted to pineapples, sugar cane, military bases, and residential subdivisions separates the two. Pearl Harbor represents the flooded lower part of this central valley. The main urban areas lie between Pearl Harbor on the west and Diamond Head on the east, with a cluster of satellite cities (Kailua/Kaneohe) across the mountains from downtown Honolulu. Other parts of the island have a decidedly rural character. Both mountain ranges are forested, although non-native plants and birds are found even at the highest reaches. Despite the heavy hand of mankind, Oahu remains a lovely island with spectacular scenic vistas for anyone willing to venture away from the city.

Many birders assume that, because of its large population and urbanization, Oahu should be avoided. Happily, such is not the case. In fact, Oahu is probably the best island for shorebirds, migratory ducks, and seabirds. Also, for better or worse, Oahu has more introduced species than any other island. Oahu has only one endemic species (Oahu Creeper), now very rare, but is the only place in the main Hawaiian Islands to see such others as Masked Booby, Gray-backed Tern, and Common Fairy-Tern.

Common and Widespread Birds

Cattle Egret
Black-crowned Night-Heron
Northern Shoveler*
Northern Pintail*
Pacific Golden-Plover*
Wandering Tattler*
Sanderling*
Ruddy Turnstone*
Rock Dove
Spotted Dove

Zebra Dove
Red-vented Bulbul
Common Myna
Japanese White-eye
Northern Cardinal
Red-crested Cardinal
House Finch
House Spar row
Nutmeg Mannikin

*seasonal

1. Tantalus/Roundtop Scenic Loop

Location: Mauka from downtown Honolulu. Detail Map A.

Access: West ern (Ewa) leg of loop (Tantalus Drive) most easily reached from Pali Highway just mauka (north) of Lunalilo Freeway. Follow signs to National Memorial Cemetery of the Pacific. Reaching the cemetery requires several turns, so be observant. Signs in this area have a habit of disappearing, but more than one route will get you where you want to go. Basically, just keep heading uphill on the slope of Punchbowl Crater and look for Puowaina Street which circles the crater on the mauka side. As you travel mauka on Puowaina, it veers to the right into the national cemetery. Keep left and you will be on Tantalus Drive.

  The eastern (Diamond Head) leg (Roundtop Drive) can be easily reached from Waikiki by taking McCully mauka across the freeway and then turning left on Wilder Avenue. Cross Punahou St. (a major thoroughfare) and take the third right (mauka) onto Makiki Street. Soon the road forks; the right is Roundtop Drive, the left is Makiki Heights Drive which will take you to Tantalus Drive, where you should turn right (mauka). You can also stay on Makiki which becomes Roundtop Drive, but I prefer to approach the loop from the Tantalus end.

Precautions: The road is steep with numerous sharp curves. Use lower gears when descending. Be mindful of other traffic and do not stop on the road around blind curves. Do not leave valuables unattended in a parked car.

Notable Species:

Common Amakihi	White-rumped Shama
Apapane	Java Sparrow
Red-whiskered Bulbul	

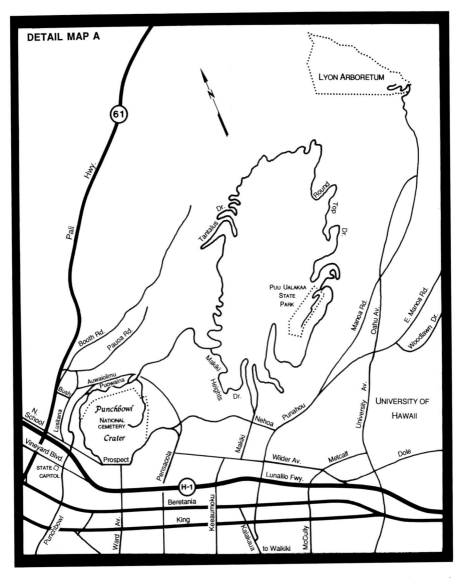

This magnificent scenic drive winds through lush rainforest and affords several spectacular views of the city of Honolulu. It is also the most accessible location for seeing the Common Amakihi on Oahu. One of the best spots is the **Punchbowl Lookout** (the third paved left-side pullout from the bottom on Tantalus Drive) where all the listed species can be found. Another worthwhile stop is **Puu Ualakaa State Park** (closed after dark) on Roundtop. The panorama of Honolulu from here is unequalled. Although Japanese Bush-Warblers are frequently heard on this drive, they are easier to

31

see elsewhere (Site 7). To find Common Amakihi, listen for their thin mewing call note. They tend to congregate around blooming trees such as eucalyptus or the red-flowered wiliwili (coralbean) that also attract great numbers of Japanese White-eyes, so picking the native birds out of the crowd can be a challenge. At peaks of bloom, Apapane sometimes wander to lower than normal elevations and can be seen here. The fact that two species of native forest birds can still be seen only ten minutes from downtown Honolulu is rather remarkable.

2. Lyon Arboretum

Location: Head of Manoa Valley at end of Manoa Road (*not* East Manoa Road) past Paradise Park. Detail Map A.

Access: Open to the public weekdays 9 am-4pm. Admission is free, but donations are appreciated. Visitors must register at the office before touring the arboretum. City buses go as far as Paradise Park.

Precautions: Paths through the arboretum are steep in places and usually muddy. Rain is frequent, so dress accordingly. Mosquitoes are sometimes a problem; carry repellent.

Notable Species: Common Amakihi
Red-vented Bulbul
Red-whiskered Bulbul
White-rumped Shama

       Lyon Arboretum, operated by the University of Hawaii Botany Department, is one of Oahu's most beautiful and least known (to the average tourist) spots. The lush vegetation and the spectacular view from Inspiration Point (see photo) are worth a visit even though most of the birds can be seen with equal ease elsewhere. However, because the birds are accustomed to people, opportunities for photography are many. This is probably the best place to get close to a White-rumped Shama and one of the few places on Oahu where one can get an eye-level view of a Common Amakihi (especially when the trees around the parking lot are in bloom). At one time, a few Hill Mynas inhabited the huge, flat-topped *Albizzia* trees above the parking area, but they have not been seen lately. Hill Mynas are not at this time known to be established anywhere on Oahu. The arboretum office has a gift shop that carries probably the best selection of books on botanical subjects in Hawaii and also carries important titles on other natural history subjects. This is a worthy operation, so please make future birders welcome by leaving a donation.

3. Waikiki

Location: Eastern Honolulu at the base of Diamond Head. Detail Map B.

Access: Probably the most accessible locality in Hawaii! Kapiolani Park is at the Diamond Head end. Fort DeRussy occupies a large block bordered on two sides by Ala Moana Boulevard and Kalakaua Avenue.

Precautions: Birders will have to put up with incredulous stares and silly questions from tourists (but you're used to that), and will have to watch out for armies of joggers in Kapiolani Park. Motorists are legally required to stop for pedestrians in marked crosswalks, and residents usually do, but beware the mainland tourist in a rental car. When birding near the archery range in Kapiolani Park, be careful to stay out of the line of fire.

Notable Species: Pacific Golden-Plover*   Common Fairy-Tern
                       Great Frigatebird   Rose-ringed Parakeet*
                       Red-whiskered Bulbul   Yellow-fronted Canary
                       Java Sparrow   Orange-cheeked Waxbill*

Almost any birder visiting Oahu will have to spend at least a little time in Waikiki, where most hotels are located. Surprisingly, this tourist mecca is actually a good birding spot and is an excellent place to start learning the common introduced birds. All of the species listed as common throughout Oahu can be seen in Waikiki, and the two species boldfaced above are most easily found here. The fairy-terns (usually called White Tern in technical bird books) nest in large trees at several sites among the hotels. They are present all year but can be unpredictable during the nonbreeding

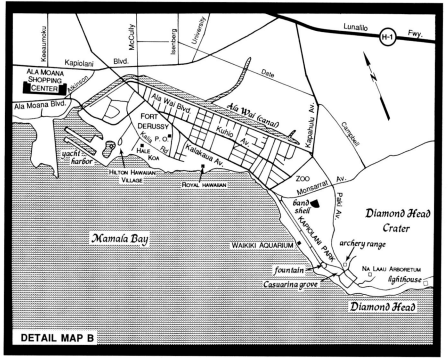

months (usually late summer through February, but variable year to year). The easiest place to find birds with eggs or chicks (no nest is built) is the large grove of ironwood (*Casuarina*) trees near the big fountain at the Diamond Head end of Kapiolani Park along Kalakaua Avenue. They also are often seen near the Waikiki Aquarium, the tennis courts along Paki Avenue, in the huge kiawe trees behind the Hale Koa Hotel at Fort DeRussy, and in the trees behind the Hilton Hawaiian Village sign at the Ala Moana-Kalia Road intersection. Most of the abundant Rock Doves in Waikiki are all white, but their loud flapping flight is quite unlike the graceful aerial maneuvers of the fairy-terns. The ironwood grove mentioned above is sometimes invaded by flocks of Rose-ringed Parakeets when the seeds are at the proper stage. Quite a few escaped parrots live in Kapiolani Park, but only this species is considered established. Yellow-fronted Canaries are most easily found in trees in Kapiolani Park. A particularly good spot for several species is the Bougainvillea-covered cliff behind the archery range at the Diamond Head end of Paki Avenue. When the grass here is high and the seeds are in the green or "milk" stage, look for Common and occasionally Orange-cheeked waxbills among the numerous Nutmeg Mannikins.

Formerly, the trail through the **Na Laau Arboretum** (trailhead marked on Makalei St. off Diamond Head Road) was an excellent place to bird. However, such species as Lavender Waxbill and Pin-tailed Whydah that once were found there have apparently died out, and the trail has not been well maintained. Rose-ringed Parakeets have been seen there lately, but are very irregular. Still, the walk up to the lookout is worth the effort for a spectacular view.

4. Paiko Lagoon

Location: Eastern Honolulu, on beach side of Kalanianaole Highway at Hawaii Kai. Detail Map C.

Access: Viewing areas open to the public. Take Lunalilo Freeway (H-1) east from downtown or Waikiki. The freeway eventually becomes Kalanianaole Highway. After passing Niu Valley Shopping Center, watch for Kuliouou Road where you should turn right. Proceed two blocks to the dead end from which you can view most of the **Paiko Lagoon State Wildlife Sanctuary**. A second access point, with less visibility but better parking, is one block east at the makai end of Bay Street (Kuliouou Beach Park).
Notable Species: Black-necked Stilt

This area is included not because it is a prime birding locality but rather because it is the kind of place where almost anything can show up. Usually little of interest is present, but over the years such rarities as Western, Glaucous, and California gulls have appeared here. It is always worth a stop on your way to somewhere else just to "check it out." At low tide, a fairly extensive mudflat has all the usual shorebirds (see Oahu list), so look for the oddball among them and you might find a diamond in the rough. In spring, Ruddy Turnstones, many of them in breeding plumage, are particularly numerous here.

5. Koko Head Regional Park

Location: Southeastern Oahu, between Hawaii Kai and Makapuu. Detail Map C.

Access: Kalanianaole Hwy. (Rt. 72) provides access to the entire area. Easily reached by bus (take Sea Life Park or Waimanalo route, No. 58).

Notable Species:	Wedge-tailed Shearwater	Great Frigatebird
	Christmas Shearwater	Gray-backed (Spectacled) Tern
	Red-footed Booby	Sooty Tern
	Red-tailed Tropicbird	Brown Noddy

This large park encompasses some of the most spectacular scenery of Oahu's dry southeastern end and some of the most visited sites for tourists. Hanauma Bay at the park's western end is probably Hawaii's most famous snorkeling spot, and is worth a stop just for the view from the parking area. Unfortunately, in recent times the bay was nearly "loved to death," its pristine character being trampled beneath the feet of hordes of visitors. Recently, restrictions to control the number of visitors have been put into effect (check with the Hawaii Visitors Bureau for details), so things may improve. The bay is not of any special interest to the birder, but if you can elbow your way into the water, you can still see numerous colorful fish up close.

The centerpiece of the park is **Koko Crater**, a large cinder cone similar geologicaly to Diamond Head. Although maps show a road into the crater, the interior is not presently accessible by car. Red-tailed Tropicbirds nest here, and can usually be observed along the highway on the makai side of the crater. A good place to look for them is the parking area for the **Halona Blowhole**. Listen for their raucous calls and look for them overhead. During spring and summer, this is also a good place to set up a spotting scope and look for seabirds offshore. Sooty Terns pass by in impressive numbers on their

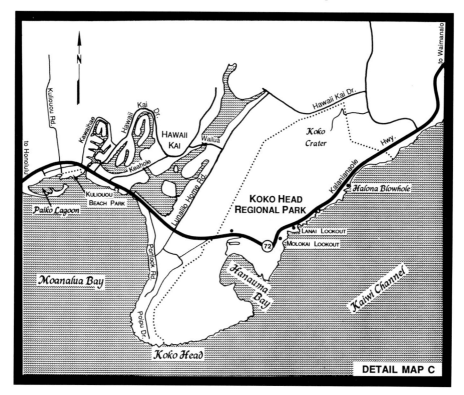

DETAIL MAP C

way to and from their nesting sites around Makapuu Point, and if you have a good scope, you should be able to pick out a few Gray-backs among them. During the breeding season (March - September) an hour to two before sunset, thousands of Wedge-tailed Shearwaters begin to appear fairly close to shore. Among them are a few Christmas Shearwaters, which can be picked out with careful study. Added bonuses include green sea-turtles in the surf below the lookout and humpback whales offshore (January-April). Theoretically, almost any of Oahu's breeding seabirds could be seen from this vantage point.

Another excellent place to set up your scope is just around the first sharp curve past Hanauma Bay, at a wide paved shoulder on the right. You can cross over the guardrail and set up on this high promontory for an excellent view with relative privacy.

6. Makapuu and Manana Island

Location: Extreme southeastern tip of Oahu, between Hanauma Bay and Waimanalo on Kalanianaole Hwy. Detail Map D.

Access: Manana Island lookout and Makapuu Beach Park are open to the public. Offshore islands are seabird sanctuaries and unauthorized landings are prohibited. The best way to visit Manana is with one of the field trips conducted from time to time by the Hawaii Audubon Society. To visit Makapuu, you can make a loop excursion from Honolulu either heading east on Lunalilo Freeway (H-1) or north on Pali Highway. Lunalilo Freeway becomes Kalanianaole Highway, which takes you to Makapuu. Kalanianaole intersects with Pali Highway at Castle Hospital, just mauka from Kailua. All areas may be reached by bus.

Notable Species:	Wedge-tailed Shearwater	Great Frigatebird
	Red-tailed Tropicbird	Sooty Tern
	Brown Booby	Brown Noddy
	Red-footed Booby	Black Noddy

This is the most accessible area on Oahu for viewing a variety of breeding seabirds. Great Frigatebirds and Red-footed Boobies are present all year, but the others listed are mostly seasonal (see seasonal chart in Introduction). **Manana Island** is an uninhabited seabird sanctuary, and during the nesting season (March-August) is home to thousands of Sooty Terns that pepper the ground and swirl over the island in a huge cloud. From shore, the spectacle is best appreciated through a spotting scope. Among the terns, look for all-white birds flying in groups of 2 or 3. These will be Red-tailed Tropicbirds cavorting in their characteristic back-pedaling display flight. Look closely, however, because a few Cattle Egrets are usually present on the island. In April, the tropicbirds frequently fly over the adjacent mainland and may even hover at eye level at the upper overlook (at the top of the hill above the beach).

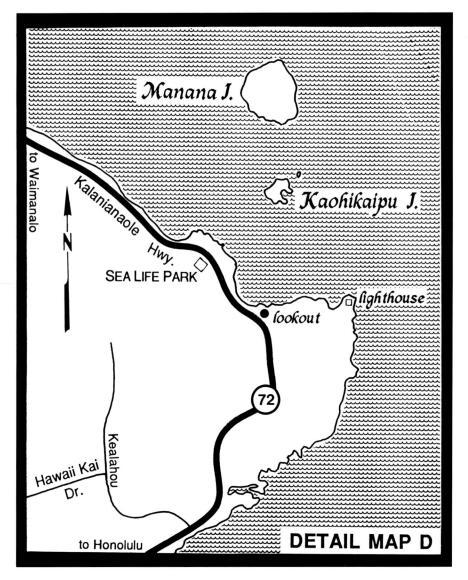

The two noddy species are difficult to sort out at a distance, but the Blacks tend to congregate in tight groups on the beach at the base of Manana Island, while the Browns are more scattered. The best vantage point for identifying the noddies is the beach park because it puts you closer to the island. For other viewing, the upper lookout is better. Wedge-tailed Shearwaters nest in burrows on Kaohikaipu Island, the relatively flat island between Manana and the mainland. They are rarely seen during midday, but look for them returning to their burrows at dusk.

Sea Life Park (admission charge) is mauka from the beach park. The exhibits and shows include the obligatory trained dolphins and other popular attractions, but the adjacent Oceanic Institute is devoted to serious research. A semi-tame colony of Red-footed Boobies, begun with a few rehabilitated injured birds, breeds in the park. Occasionally Brown Boobies and rarely Masked Boobies hang around the colony.

The trip to Makapuu is worth it for scenery alone. Between Makapuu and Pali Highway you pass Waimanalo Beach, possibly the most beautiful on Oahu, and Mt. Olomana with its twin spires, all with a backdrop of the fluted windward *pali*.

7. Kawainui Regional Park

Location: Mauka from the town of Kailua, windward Oahu. Detail Map E.

Access: Kawainui Marsh is visible from many surrounding roads and highways, but finding a vantage point that will allow the birder to set up a scope and view open water is something of a challenge. One good spot is directly behind Castle Memorial Hospital at the intersection of Kailua Road and Kalanianaole Highway. Turn onto Ulukahiki Street and go behind the hospital where the road turns sharply to the left. On the right is a vacant lot where the trees do not obstruct the view of the marsh. You will have to cross a barbed wire fence, so presumably this is private property but as of this writing no threatening signs are apparent. A spotting scope is essential. If you see something from here on the open water and want a closer look, you can try taking Quarry Road (at Kailua Drive-in Theater mauka from Castle Hospital on Kalanianaole Highway) and "bushwhacking" through the woods to the edge of the marsh. There are presently no trails, but the strip of scrubby woods is narrow.

Precautions: Virtually all access points to the marsh are on private property, so if anyone is around, ask permission to set up your scope. I have personally never been hassled in the area. Scrambling through the woods along Quarry Road is strictly "at your own risk."

Notable Species:	Great Frigatebird	**Common Moorhen**
	Black-crowned Night-Heron	**Hawaiian Coot**
	Koloa (Hawaiian Duck)	Black-necked Stilt

Kawainui ("The Big Water") **Marsh** was a prehistoric fishpond for raising mullet. When it fell into disuse, it gradually began to silt in and become choked with vegetation so that only a few small patches of open water remained, and its value as a wetland slowly diminished. In the past, when more open water was present, wintering ducks were numerous here. Various conservation and Hawaiian heritage organizations campaigned for years for restoration of Kawainui to a more ecologically productive state. In 1990, their efforts finally resulted in the passage of a bill to establish the regional park. As of this writing the marsh (on many maps it is called a "swamp," but marsh is more accurate) is still badly overgrown and deteriorating, but as the master plan for the new park is implemented in coming years, the habitat should improve and birding should be greatly enhanced. The plan calls for a major wildlife sanctuary for endangered water birds and hiking trails to improve viewing. In 1991, an area of open water along the western side of the park was created by blasting, and migratory ducks have already been seen using the area.

Migratory ducks can be expected at Kawainui between September and April. Most of them are Northern Pintail and Northern Shoveler, but such rarities as Redhead and Red-breasted Merganser have turned up here. The muddy pasture below the observation point behind Castle Hospital is presently a good place to look for Common Snipe and possibly other shorebirds.

8. Kaneohe Marine Corps Air Station

Location: Windward Oahu on the Mokapu Peninsula. Detail Map E.

Access: Closed to the general public, but arrangements can be made to visit the birding sites on the base. The easiest way to visit is with an organized group that can make the advance arrangements for you. For information, write to the Joint Public Affairs Officer, Marine Corps Air Station, Kaneohe Bay, HI 96863-5001 or call 257-2170. Visits to the booby colony in Ulupau Crater must be made in the late afternoon after activities on the nearby firing range have ceased for the day. For birding, that is the best time anyway because the light is then at your back. To reach the base from Honolulu, take the Pali Highway toward Kailua (north). At the first traffic light after you pass through the tunnels and descend on the other side, turn left onto Kamehameha Highway (Rt. 83). Look for signs to H-3, a new freeway under construction. Turn right onto the freeway which will take you directly to the main entrance of the base. An alternate route is to take Likelike Highway over the mountains to Kaneohe where the road becomes Kaneohe Bay Drive. This eventually connects with H-3 just outside the base.

Notable Species:

Laysan Albatross	**Gray-backed Tern**
Masked Booby	Sooty Tern
Brown Booby	Brown Noddy
Red-footed Booby	Black Noddy
Great Frigatebird	Black-necked Stilt

The **Kaneohe Marine Corps Air Station (MCAS)** occupies the greater part of the **Mokapu Peninsula** that juts out between the towns of Kaneohe and Kailua. The most important place for birders on the peninsula is **Ulupau Crater** at the makai end.

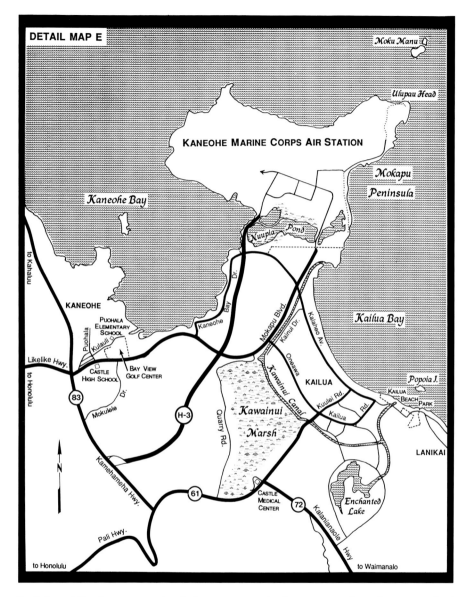

DETAIL MAP E

Red-footed Boobies nest in haole koa trees inside the crater and can be approached closely. Birds are present in the colony all year, but most breeding takes place between April and November. The colony attracts large numbers of kleptoparasitic Great Frigatebirds, which nest on **Moku Manu**, a steep-sided, flat-topped island that can be viewed from the top of the outer rim of the crater (**Ulupau Head**). Moku Manu is also a breeding site for thousands of Sooty Terns, as well as Brown Boobies and Brown Noddies, and is the only place in the main Hawaiian Islands where Gray-backed Terns and Masked Boobies (a few) nest. With the aid of a spotting scope, all of these species can be seen from Ulupau Head. Check the small sandy beach on the near side of Moku Manu for Hawaiian monk seals. A few Christmas Shearwaters also nest on Moku Manu, but come and go at night so are rarely seen from Ulupau Head. Both Brown and Black Noddies nest on ledges of the steep cliff below your feet as you stand on Ulupau Head. Comparison of the two is easy as they fly below with a backdrop of deep blue water. Recently, Laysan Albatrosses have frequented the area. They sometimes land in the grassy central part of the crater, but have not yet attempted to nest.

Another place worth visiting is a group of ponds on the mauka end of the peninsula. **Nuupia Pond** and several smaller ponds are now carefully protected and managed by the Marine Corps, with help from the Fish and Wildlife Service, for the benefit of endangered freshwater birds. Black-necked Stilts nest on artificial islands in the ponds, and Black-crowned Night-herons feed along the edges. Flocks of Black Noddies frequently forage over the area. The shallows and mudflats are excellent for shorebirds during spring and fall. These ponds have a history of producing rarities, so they should always be checked. Recently a Crested Tern, first for Hawaii and the AOU Check-list area, overwintered here and was observed by many.

9. Kualoa Regional Park

Location: Windward Oahu between Kaneohe Bay to the south and Kahana Bay to the north.

Access: Park open to the public. Take Kamehameha Highway (Rt. 83) north from

Kaneohe (the first left off Likelike Highway as it descends from Wilson Tunnel) and head north. From numerous points you can see Mokolii Island (Chinaman's Hat), a familiar landmark just offshore from the park. The park entrance is on the right and is well marked by a large sign.

Notable Species: Black-necked Stilt
Pacific Golden-Plover
Ruddy Turnstone

Although not a major birding locality, this park is worth a stop on your way to other sites because of its potential for turning up something rare. In April, Pacific Golden-Plovers and Ruddy Turnstones, newly resplendent in their breeding attire, use the broad grassy lawns in the park as a staging ground for their northward migration and can be present in the hundreds. **Apua Pond** (shown above), a small shallow body of water at the far end of the parking lot, supports a few Black-necked Stilts and should be a good place to look for peeps and other shorebirds. The pond is separated from the main part of the park by a stone wall, the top of which provides an excellent vantage point for the birder.

10. Laie Point

Location: Windward Oahu in the town of Laie.

Access: Open to the public. Take Anemoku Street, the only one that heads makai in Laie, across from the shopping center between the Polynesian Cultural Center and the Mormon Temple. Anemoku doglegs and intersects with Naupaka Street where you should turn right. A parking area is a short distance ahead at the point.

Notable Species: Wedge-tailed Shearwater Brown Booby
Christmas Shearwater Black Noddy
Masked Booby Brown Noddy
Red-footed Booby

Because it juts out to the edge of the reef line, Laie Point is an excellent place to watch for seabirds that usually fly too far offshore to be identified. Most of the species that breed on Moku Manu (see Site 7) pass by the point on their way to and from the colony. This is one of the few places where one has any chance of seeing a Christmas Shearwater from land. Look for them at dawn and dusk. Wedge-tailed Shearwaters nest on Moku Auia, the flat island visible about a mile to the north of the point. Look for them late in the afternoon flying past Laie Point. A spotting scope is not essential but is very helpful. Rock Doves frequently perch on the offshore rocks here, and seem a little more "countable" than the white ones in Kapiolani Park.

11. Amorient Aquafarm and Kii Ponds

Location: Windward Oahu just north of town of Kahuku and south of Turtle Bay Resort. Detail Map F.

Access: Amorient Aquafarm is closed to public entry, but because of an extra-wide shoulder, virtually the entire area can be viewed from the main highway. The Kii Ponds are the larger unit of **James Campbell National Wildlife Refuge** located between the southern portion of the aquafarm and the beach. It is closed to all public use during the nesting season (February-September) but visits can sometimes be arranged at other times (fall is best for shorebirds and ducks anyway). At present, arrangements to visit the refuge must be made through the Refuge Manager by mail (U. S. Fish and Wildlife Service, Federal Bldg., Rm. 5302; P. O. Box 50167, Honolulu HI 96850) or phone (808/541-1201). Access usually depends on the availability of someone to accompany the visitor. The refuge manager can provide names of individuals who have permits to escort visitors. Some organized birding tours also visit this site. Plans are in the works to open a public viewing point in the refuge, so future access may be simpler. The refuge entrance road is just south of a bridge over a drainage canal between Kahuku Sugar Mill and the aquafarm.

Precautions: Traffic on Kamehameha Hwy. is often heavy and drivers are often rubbernecking as they pass the aquafarm. Exercise extreme caution when birding along the

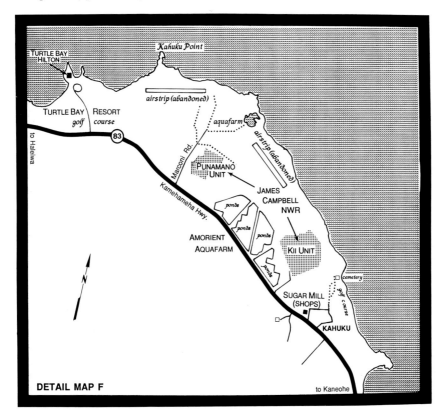

road. Visitors to James Campbell NWR should be mindful of the refuge's purpose, to provide nesting habitat for endangered water birds. The refuge is regularly patrolled, so walking in without prior arrangements could result in arrest for trespassing.

Notable Species:

Black-crowned Night-Heron	**Hawaiian Coot**
Fulvous Whistling-Duck	Black-necked Stilt
Canada Goose	Lesser Yellowlegs
Green-winged Teal	**Bristle-thighed Curlew**
Koloa (Hawaiian Duck)	Sharp-tailed Sandpiper
Garganey	Short-eared Owl
Eurasian Wigeon	Common Waxbill
Common Pheasant	**Red Avadavat**
Common Moorhen	Chestnut Mannikin

James Campbell NWR was created to preserve the wetland habitat of **Kii Pond**, formerly a settling basin for the now-defunct Kahuku Sugar Mill. It and the adjacent fresh and saltwater ponds of **Amorient Aquafarm** comprise one of the prime birding sites in the Hawaiian Islands. The two adjacent wetlands provide in abundance a habitat that is rare in the islands. Consequently, rare migratory waterfowl and shorebirds are drawn to it. Almost any species on the Hawaii checklist could show up here; those listed above are of nearly annual occurrence. Every winter a few stray gulls of various species hang around these ponds. All of Hawaii's breeding freshwater birds are here in large numbers, including the Fulvous Whistling-Duck, a recent arrival. A complicating factor is that the owners of Amorient Aquafarm have "decorated" the operation with ornamental waterfowl (everything from Australian Black Swans to various colorful shelducks to pot-bellied barnyard geese). Sometimes these birds wander onto the refuge. None of them, of course, are "countable." As far as anyone knows, the only species that has begun to breed is the Mallard (the Amorient folks claim not to have brought in the whistling-ducks), which has interbred with the native Koloa. This latter development is particularly unfortunate because it could lead to genetic swamping of the Hawaiian bird.

12. Punamano Pond

Location: Windward Oahu just south of Turtle Bay Resort. Detail Map F.

Access: This pond is a disjunct unit of **James Campbell NWR** and, although closed to entry, can be viewed without trespassing. Take Marconi Road (the only public paved road that heads makai off Kamehameha Highway between Turtle Bay Resort and Amorient Aquafarm; it follows a row of powerlines along a chain-link fence) and turn right at the first opportunity. Follow this road to a locked gate. Park in this area but be sure not to block the gate or the road. Just before the gate, a dirt road heads to the right and to another gate. Walk to the right at the second gate and follow this track about a hundred yards. You will see the pond on the left.

Notable Species:

Koloa (Hawaiian Duck)	**Japanese Bush-Warbler**
Common Moorhen	Common Waxbill
Hawaiian Coot	

Punamano Pond has the same potential for rare ducks as the previous site. Waterfowl often move between it and other ponds in the area. An added bonus here is the presence of many Japanese Bush-Warblers in the surrounding thickets of haole koa. For some reason, these birds are not as shy as they are in other localities and may sometimes be seen sitting up in dead snags above the thicker foliage. Playing a tape recording of the bird's song will virtually guarantee a good look, even in seasons when they are not singing regularly. These same thickets and edges usually also produce Common Waxbills.

13. Haleiwa and the North Shore

Location: North shore of Oahu from Haleiwa to Turtle Bay. Detail Map G.

Access: All areas open to the public and reached via Kamehameha Highway (Rt. 83). The picturesque town of Haleiwa ("Frigatebird house") is located at the "notch" of the North Shore and can be reached directly from Honolulu by taking H-1 west to H-2, then north to Rt. 99.

Precautions: Traffic is very heavy in this area , especially on weekends and holidays. Watch for pedestrians; most are preoccupied with the beach and surfing and pay little attention to passing cars. If you see a bird offshore, pull off the road to view it.

Notable Species:

Laysan Albatross	Great Frigatebird
Brown Booby	Hawaiian Coot
Red-footed Booby	

Oahu's North Shore is one of the world's premier surfing localities. One of the reasons is that the area lacks an offshore fringing reef and waves break onshore. Thus deep water is relatively close in, and seabirds sometimes come quite close to the beach. Laysan Albatrosses are uncommon but regular sights in this area January-August. Boobies sometimes perch on buoys and other structures in Haleiwa Boat Harbor, and Great Frigatebirds are often seen overhead. **Loko Ea Pond** on the mauka side of the highway on the eastern edge of Haleiwa usually harbors a few Hawaiian Coots and is a good place to look for diving ducks such as scaup during the winter months. The parking lot of a gas station-food mart provides a convenient and safe place from which to view the pond. Northeast of Haleiwa at Waimea Bay lies **Waimea Falls Park** (entrance fee). This privately operated park features botanical gardens and numerous exotic birds (none countable). Red Junglefowl have been reintroduced here, but whether they can be considered truly wild is moot.

14. Waialua Lotus Ponds

Location: In the "notch" of Oahu's North Shore, near Haleiwa. Detail Map G.

Access: Most easily reached from the traffic circle south of Haleiwa (this is where Kamehameha Highway changes from Rt. 99 to Rt. 83) by taking Waialua Beach Road. Watch for Haleiwa Road to the right. Directly across from this intersection, almost like a continuation of Haleiwa Road, is a dirt track that leads alongside the ponds which are visible from the highway.

Precautions: The area is on private land, but is not posted and birders have never been hassled. For least disturbance of birds, stay in your vehicle. Do not walk on the levees between ponds or disturb the aquacultural operations in any way.

Notable Species: Common Moorhen   Red Avadavat
                         Black-necked Stilt   Chestnut Mannikin
                         Common Waxbill

       This is a small but interesting locality where one can get quite close to both stilts and moorhens. It is an excellent photographic opportunity. During fall migration (September-November), look for less common shorebirds among the Sanderlings, turnstones, tattlers, and Pacific Golden-Plovers. This should be a good spot for peeps. The ponds exist for the production of lotus root for the oriental food market. The small finches listed above will mostly be fly-overs here.

15. Pearl Harbor Area

Location: South-central Oahu, west of Honolulu Airport.

Access: This large area is well served by highways (almost any map will do to get you around) but unfortunately most of the good birding areas are off-limits to the public. The several small tracts that comprise Pearl Harbor National Wildlife Refuge can be visited if you are escorted by someone who holds a permit to conduct such tours. For an individual, the best thing to do is to write ahead to the Refuge Manager (P. O. Box 50167, Honolulu, HI 96850) and inquire about access. Waipio Peninsula (see below) is at present totally inaccessible.

Precautions: If you are the intrepid type who views "No Trespassing" signs as a challenge, be warned that the U. S. Navy has been very obnoxious lately in seeing to it that no one visits Waipio Peninsula. They could make life very unpleasant for you.

Notable Species:

Koloa (Hawaiian Duck)	Eurasian Skylark
Hawaiian Coot	**Common Waxbill**
Black-necked Stilt	**Red Avadavat**
Lesser Yellowlegs	**Chestnut Mannikin**
Long-billed Dowitcher	

Pearl Harbor, with its deep water port, has been in the hands of the U. S. Navy over a century. It is divided into three branches called East, Middle, and West Lochs. Middle and West Lochs are separated by **Waipio Peninsula**. For many years, the peninsula has been leased to the Oahu Sugar Company and has been used for both growing and processing sugar cane. The settling basins for this operation provide extensive wetland habitats and mudflats that not only support large numbers of the endangered

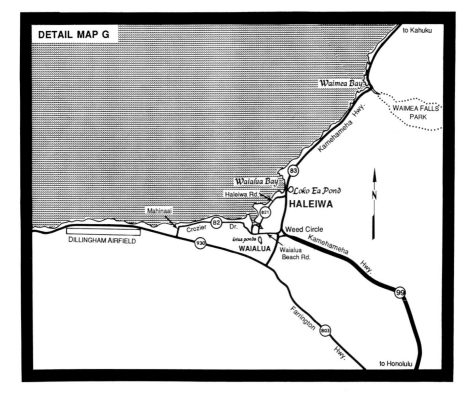

Hawaiian freshwater birds, but are one of the premier "migrant traps" in the islands. Waipio has produced as many as half of the rarities and accidentals on the Hawaii state list. For years, birders were tolerated in the area, but recently both Oahu Sugar and the U. S. Navy have tightened their grip and have made it nearly impossible for even long-time local birders to visit this important area. Until this attitude changes, the visiting birder should forget Waipio. I include it here because the locality appears so often in the ornithological literature and to call attention to what I consider to be a very short-sighted dog-in-the-manger policy on the part of the Navy. Rather than establish a refuge in this most important wetland locality in Hawaii, the U. S. Fish and Wildlife Service has had to settle for the few tiny parcels in peripheral areas that now are included in the **Pearl Harbor National Wildlife Refuge.** Still, the refuge is important in the preservation of native freshwater birds. Also, the **Honouliuli Unit** has become an important migrant trap in its own right. It has recently yielded such rarities as Common and Least terns, Greater Yellowlegs, Solitary Sandpiper, Brant, Garganey, and Eurasian Wigeon. Though difficult to arrange, it is not impossible to visit this area outside the nesting season. The Refuge Manager can provide names of current permittees who could take you there, but keep in mind these are mostly persons who are not professional tour guides. They may or may not be available and you should expect to provide your own transportation. One of the biggest problems for birders at Honouliuli Unit is that birds often take off and fly the short distance over to now-inaccessible Waipio Peninsula.

The estrildid finches mentioned above reach their greatest abundance in the Pearl Harbor area. For many years, Waipio Peninsula was the only place to see Red Avadavats on Oahu, but they are now more widespread. All three species listed can be found anywhere in the vicinity of Pearl Harbor in the weedy edges of canefields. They usually are in large flocks and are best differentiated initially by their distinctive call notes.

16. Aiea Ridge Trail

Location: South-central Oahu, above Pearl Harbor.

Access: The trail is open to the public for day use. From Honolulu, take Lunalilo Freeway (H-1) west and bear left on Moanalua Road (Rt. 78) marked "Aiea." Follow subsequent signs for Aiea, take the right turn onto Aiea Heights Drive, and follow it to its end at Keaiwa Heiau State Recreation Area. Take the upper trailhead marked "Aiea Loop Trail" and proceed mauka. At a point where the trail turns sharply to the right and begins to double back, an unmarked trail heads mauka off the loop. This is Aiea Ridge Trail.

Precautions: The trail is narrow, rugged, and often muddy, especially at the upper reaches. Wear good supportive footwear and protective clothing (vegetation, some of it with thorns, often overhangs the trail). Be prepared for rain.

Notable Species: Japanese Bush-Warbler   **Oahu Creeper** (see below)
White-rumped Shama   Apapane
Common Amakihi

The Aiea Ridge Trail is one of the best trails to get the birder into high-elevation forest on Oahu. The trail eventually reaches the crest of the Koolau Range at one of its higher points. The forest at the upper end is wind-blown and scrubby, so the best birding is actually below the highest elevations. Although introduced plants are evident throughout the area, the forest is dominated by native plants such as ohia, koa, olapa, and ieie. Apapane and Common Amakihi are fairly common. This is one of the best places to look for the rare and elusive Oahu Creeper, Oahu's only endemic species. Several recent sightings of this bird have been in **North Halawa Valley**, just below and to the southeast of Aiea Ridge. The valley is now closed to entry because of construction of the new H-3 freeway, but presumably one's chances of finding the creeper are better at higher elevations anyway. Probably many observers overlook this species because it closely resembles the Common Amakihi in plumage and feeding behavior (contrary to some older literature, it does *not* creep like a nuthatch). Listen for a distinctive sharp *chirk*, similar to the call of the Maui Creeper. Be prepared for disappointment; only a few people have seen this bird in the past two decades.

17. Sand Island State Recreation Area

Location: Sand Island in Honolulu Harbor.

Access: Park open to the public 7 AM-7:45 PM daily. The access road turns makai off Nimitz Highway just east of its intersection with H-1. (Nimitz Highway is continuous with Ala Moana Boulevard east of downtown.) The sign reads "Sand Island Road/U. S. Coast Guard Station." Take this road all the way to its end at the beach park.

Notable Species: Brown Booby   **Pomarine Jaeger**
                        Red-footed Booby   Sooty Tern
                        Great Frigatebird   Common Fairy-Tern

Sand Island is an easily accessible place from which to view seabirds with a spotting scope. During the winter months (October-May) Pomarine Jaegers can nearly always be seen from here, and occasionally they come in quite close to shore. Most of the birds listed will be quite far out, however, but nevertheless identifiable. The park has a tantalizing lookout tower that would probably be a good vantage point but it is closed. Because of its proximity to Honolulu Harbor, Sand Island is a good place to look for ship-assisted vagrants. European Starling and Great-tailed Grackle have turned up here recently.

Molokai

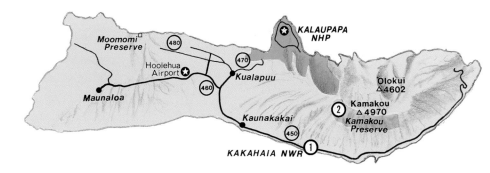

MOLOKAI

Molokai, the smallest and least developed of Hawaii's most frequently-visited islands, is roughly rectangular, with the western two-thirds low and relatively flat. The eastern end rises to a little over 4,000 feet. Deeply eroded valleys cutting into the mountain mass from the north shore produce some of the most striking vistas in the islands, including the world's tallest sea cliffs. The low, isolated Kalaupapa Peninsula juts northward at about the midpoint of the island. It was once a leper colony, and a few patients still live there, but it recently has been incorporated into **Kalaupapa National Historical Park**. Dense native forest still remains on Molokai's higher elevations, but its birds are mostly gone. Most of the island's endemics such as the Black Mamo, last seen in 1908, and the Kakawahie, last seen in 1964, are believed extinct. Nevertheless one, the Olomao, still just barely survives (see Site 2). This sad state of affairs is all the more unfortunate because the island is so beautiful and so relatively untouched by civilization.

Common Birds

Cattle Egret	Common Myna
Black-crowned Night-Heron	Japanese White-eye
Pacific Golden-Plover*	Northern Cardinal
Wandering Tattler*	Red-crested Cardinal
Ruddy Turnstone*	House Finch
Rock Dove	House Sparrow
Spotted Dove	Nutmeg Mannikin
Zebra Dove	

*seasonal

1. Kakahaia National Wildlife Refuge

Location: South coast of Molokai, about five miles east of Kaunakakai.

Access: Although the refuge is closed to the public, it can be viewed from the main highway (Rt. 450), which passes right through it. Look for a parking area on the mauka side of the highway. On the makai side, Kakahaia Beach County Park provides parking and a picnic area from which much of the refuge can also be seen.

Notable Species: Hawaiian Coot
                         Black-necked Stilt
       This refuge was established for the two above-named endangered species, but it also provides habitat for other species attracted to fresh water. Such habitat is scarce on Molokai, so Kakahaia Pond is something of a magnet for stray waterfowl, gulls, terns, and shorebirds. The best months to look for rarities are October-April.

2. Kamakou Preserve

Location: Higher elevations of eastern Molokai.

Access: Closed to the public. Visits to the preserve must be arranged through the Preserve Manager at P. O. Box 40, Kualapuu, HI 96757 or phone (808) 567-6680. The Nature Conservancy of Hawaii conducts regular hikes into the preserve for its members.

Notable Species: Olomao
Japanese Bush-Warbler
Common Amakihi
Iiwi
Apapane

      The Kamakou Preserve of The Nature Conservancy of Hawaii was established as a refuge for rare native plants and animals including birds. Its most important resident is the Olomao, arguably the rarest surviving native bird in Hawaii today. Estimates are that fewer than twenty individuals survive. Sightings of Olomao are few and far between; it has never been sighted on a Nature Conservancy hike. The last sighting of the scarlet Kakawahie (Molokai Creeper), now believed extinct, was in the area now included in the preserve. Diligent searches for the Kakawahie in recent years have been unproductive. Even the "common" honeycreepers are rare in eastern Molokai. For the birder this is a particularly sad place because the habitat looks nearly pristine, with few alien plants. Yet, it is nearly birdless except for Japanese Bush-Warblers, which recently invaded Molokai from Oahu. Apparently, Molokai is not high enough to provide a sufficiently large disease-free upland refuge for native birds.

Maui

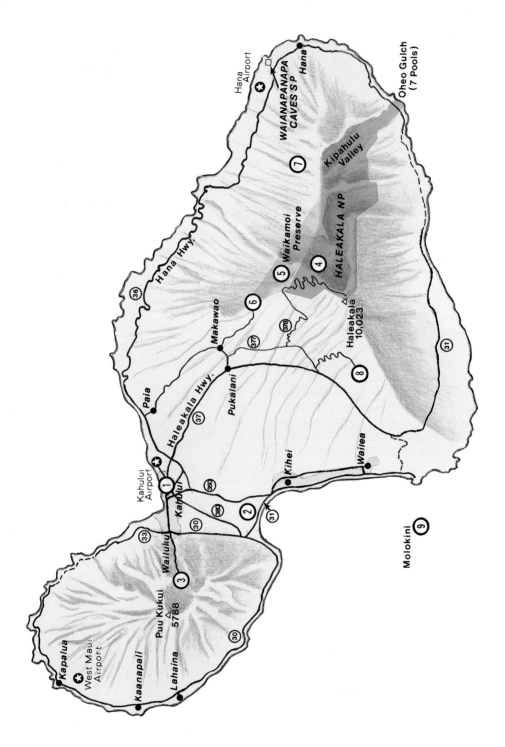

Hana Airport

Hana

WAIANAPANAPA CAVES S'P

⑦

Oheo Gulch (7 Pools)

Kipahulu Valley

Waikamoi Preserve

⑤ ④

HALEAKALA NP

Hana Hwy.

㊱

⑥

Makawao

378

Haleakala 10,023 △

⑧

377

31

Paia

Haleakala Hwy.

37

Pukalani

Kihei

Wailea

Kahului Airport

① Kahului

360

②

31

③⑥⑧

30

Molokini ⑨

33

Wailuku

③

Puu Kukui 5788 △

30

Kapalua

West Maui Airport

Kaanapali

Lahaina

MAUI

Maui, Hawaii's second largest island, is formed by two mountains joined by a low isthmus. East Maui is dominated by Haleakala Volcano, the third highest peak in the islands. West Maui is geologically older and more eroded, with deep valleys and steep slopes. For the birder, West Maui holds little of interest but Haleakala is a must on any itinerary. The political center of Maui County, which includes Molokai, Lanai, and Kahoolawe, is the town of Wailuku. The main airport is in Kahului, adjacent to Wailuku in the central isthmus of the island. A second major airport has recently opened to service the resorts at Kaanapali in West Maui, and a small commuter airstrip serves Hana. For the birder, the Kahului Airport is the most convenient. Most hotels are in the Kaanapali-Lahaina area (the largest tourist development) and the Kihei-Makena area. A few are located in Kahului (mostly local clientele) and Hana. Rental cars are available at both major airports. For birding Haleakala, the Kihei and Kahului locations are more convenient. One of the best accommodations for birders is Kula Lodge (RR1, Box 475, Kula, Maui, HI 96790; 878-1535), a small rustic hotel in the village of Kula in the "upcountry" region on the lower slopes of Haleakala. It is isolated from the major resorts, has a first-class restaurant, wonderful sunset views, and will save you at least an hour of driving at either end of a day's birding on the mountain.

Common and Widespread Birds

Cattle Egret	Rock Dove
Black-crowned Night-Heron	Spotted Dove
Northern Shoveler*	Zebra Dove
Northern Pintail*	Common Myna
Gray Francolin	Japanese White-eye
Pacific Golden-Plover*	Northern Mockingbird
Wandering Tattler*	Northern Cardinal
Sanderling*	House Finch
Ruddy Turnstone*	House Sparrow

*seasonal

1. Kanaha Pond

Location: In Kahului, less than a mile from Kahului Airport. Detail Map H.

Access: Open to the public. From the airport, follow signs for Kahului and keep bearing to the right. The parking lot is just beyond the turn-off for Lahaina (do not make the turn). From the main part of town, take the Hana Highway (Rt 36) east. Very soon you will see the pond on the left across the divided highway. Take the left turn toward the airport (Rt 396). The parking lot is visible from this intersection. A paved path leads to a central observation area with a covered stone kiosk.

Precautions: Recent widening of the highway has greatly restricted the width of the shoulder that is available for viewing the side ponds (see below). There is still room to set up a scope, but when birding in groups be sure not to stray onto the pavement and keep in mind that nearly every passing idiot will feel the need to honk, just to startle you.

Notable Species:

Black-crowned Night-Heron	Osprey
Green-winged Teal	Hawaiian Coot
American Wigeon	Black-necked Stilt
Eurasian Wigeon	Long-billed Dowitcher

Kanaha Pond Wildlife Sanctuary is a state preserve established primarily for the protection of Black-necked Stilts (Hawaiian subspecies) but which also provides habitat for many other wetland species. The resident birds have become used to people and will pose quite close for photographs. Like many such ponds in the islands, Kanaha is a "migrant trap" where many unusual species have turned up over the years. From October to April it harbors flocks of all the usual wintering ducks, as well as a sprinkling of rarer ones. Eurasian Wigeons are not present every year, but they are regular enough here to warrant searching every group of wigeon. Likewise, this is one of the best spots for teal of several species, the Green-winged being the most frequent. Both Blue-winged Teal and Garganey are nearly annual visitors, so all teal-size ducks should be examined closely. Ospreys are not always present but have turned up here more frequently than anywhere else on Maui. Scan the trees on the far side of the pond from the observation area for easily overlooked perched Ospreys. The best area for shorebirds, which almost always include a few Long-billed Dowitchers and, during spring and fall, Sharp-tailed Sandpipers, is easy to miss because it is not visible from the parking lot or central kiosk. To view this area (a scope is almost essential), walk along the shoulder of the highway a few yards toward the airport from the parking lot. The best spot for viewing is just as the small side ponds and mudflats become visible.

Near Kanaha Pond is another spot that can at times be very productive for shorebirds. The **Hansen Road ponds**, as they are known locally, are two canefield settling basins located adjacent to the landfill on Hansen Road. To reach them you can either take the road to Lahaina (the one you passed up on the way to Kanaha Pond from the airport) and turn left toward the Puunene sugar mill, or take Puunene Avenue out of Kahului. As you near the mill, turn left on Hansen Road, a small paved road easy to miss. There is a sign here indicating the direction to the landfill. If you reach the mill where the road veers to the right, you have gone too far. Hansen Road winds through

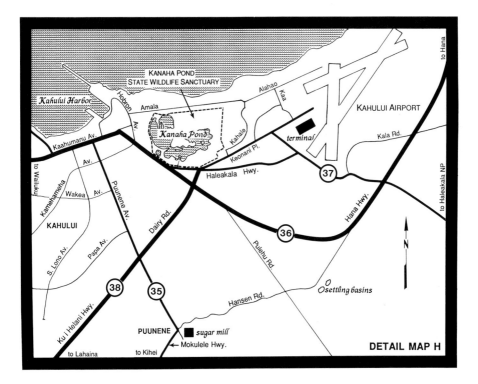

the mill complex and then straightens out among the canefields. Watch for Orange-cheeked Waxbills in weedy edges. Go past the road to the landfill and immediately look for a dirt track to the right that will take you up onto the obvious earthen mounds on the right. These "roads" change from time to time, and often are very muddy. If it has been raining recently, it would be a good idea to park below and walk up the dirt tracks. Use discretion to avoid getting stuck. Bearing to the left once atop the mounds, you should see one or two shallow ponds on the right. Sometimes both ponds are completely dry, sometimes too full to have mudflats; their productivity for birding depends entirely on luck. At their best, the ponds can be an excellent place to look for peeps, especially Least Sandpipers.

2. Kealia Pond

Location: The southern part of Maui's central isthmus, on Maalaea Bay. Detail Map I.

Access: The pond lies along North Kihei Road (Rt. 31) between Rt. 30 and Rt. 350. From Kahului, take Puunene Road south to the sugar mill at Puunene and continue to the right (no turn required) on Mokulele Highway (Rt. 350) to the first major intersection (at Kihei). Turn right and begin looking for the pond on the right. From Lahaina and Kaanapali, take Rt 30 toward Kahului and turn right onto Rt 31 just past the village of Maalaea. You will first see some shallow pools (sometimes dry) on the right between the road and the beach, then the pond will be visible on the left. Access points with room to park are at the extreme eastern and western ends of the pond, with one in the middle where you can drive a few yards on a dirt track off the highway mauka. It is possible (though not usually necessary for good viewing) to walk to the north shore of the eastern end of the pond on two gated dirt roads off Rt 350. One leads to a now-defunct aquafarming project.

Precautions: Traffic on Kihei Road can be horrendous, so exercise extreme caution both driving and walking. The walk to the edge of the pond can be muddy, so appropriate footwear should be available.

Notable Species: Same as for Kanaha Pond (Maui 1).

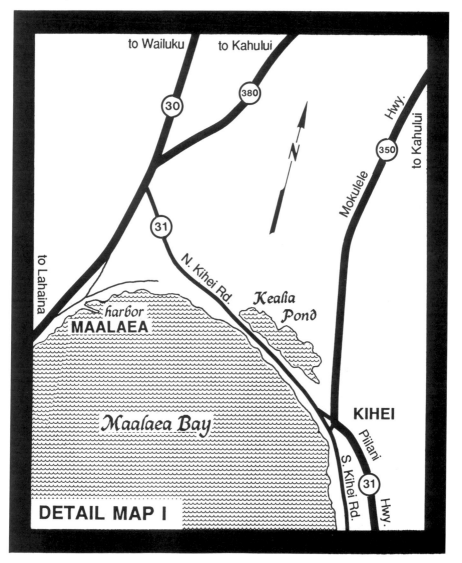

Kealia is a large shallow pond slated to become a national wildlife refuge if ongoing litigation by the U. S. Fish and Wildlife Service is successful. It is home to many Hawaiian Coots (endangered) and is probably the best place on Maui to look for migratory ducks. Large flocks of Northern Pintails and Northern Shovelers provide a fine spectacle during the winter months, and every year something unusual shows up. Recent rarities have included Eurasian Wigeon, Redhead, Garganey, and the first Hawaii record of Common Merganser. This is also a good place to look for rare herons and egrets. Cattle Egrets maintain a huge roost on the north side of the eastern end of the pond, and native Black-crowned Night-Herons are also abundant. Perhaps because of this concentration, rarities such as Great Blue Heron, Great Egret, and Snowy Egret are occasionally found at Kealia. When low water levels coincide with migration periods, Kealia becomes a major "migrant trap" for shorebirds such as Black-bellied Plover, Whimbrel, and Lesser Yellowlegs. Recent rarities have included Dunlin, Western Sandpiper, and Rufous-necked Stint. Especially when the main pond is full, be sure to examine the shallow pools between the road and the beach at the western end. Ospreys, which can be difficult to find in Hawaii, are at Kealia almost every winter and probably cruise between here and Kanaha Pond on the other side of the Maui isthmus. Laughing and Ring-billed gulls are fairly regular in winter and several other gulls, including Franklin's and Bonaparte's, have turned up recently.

3. Iao Valley State Park

Location: In the heart of West Maui, above Wailuku.

Access: Open to the public. From the Kahului airport, follow Rt. 32 through Kahului and Wailuku into Iao Valley (bear right at the Y above Wailuku). The road dead-ends at the park. From West Maui or Kihei, take Rt. 30 north to Wailuku and turn left onto Rt. 32.

Notable Species: White-tailed Tropicbird
Common Amakihi

Iao Valley is not an important birding area, but is included here because most visitors to Maui will want to see it. The park surrounds a volcanic plug known as the Iao Needle. A paved path makes a loop through the park. Japanese White-eyes are abundant and conspicuous, and occasionally a Common Amakihi may wander down to this unusually low-elevation site. Look for Wandering Tattlers along the rocky stream. At times, White-tailed Tropicbirds can be seen circling against the cliffs surrounding the "needle."

4. Haleakala National Park

Location: East Maui, encompassing the summit of Haleakala, Kipahulu Valley, and the Seven Pools area along the south coast. Detail Map J.

Access: The park is open daily to the public and requires an entrance fee (Golden Eagle passes accepted). To reach the summit area, head east from Kahului on Haleakala Highway (Rt. 37) and follow the signs. Two left turns, one just above Pukalani, the other just above Kula Lodge, are well marked. The Seven Pools area is reached by the Hana Highway (Rt. 36) which becomes Piilani Highway (Rt. 31) past the town of Hana. This route also is well marked. For schedules of hikes and other activities, write to The Superintendent, Haleakala National Park, Box 369, Makawao HI 96768.

Precautions: Both the Hana Highway and Haleakala Crater Road have innumerable twists and turns. Persons susceptible to car sickness should take precautions. The last gas station before the drive to the summit is in Pukalani, so be sure you have enough for the round trip.

Notable Species:

Hawaiian Petrel	Eurasian Skylark
White-tailed Tropicbird	Red-billed Leiothrix
Nene	Northern Mockingbird
Common Pheasant	**Common Amakihi**
Chukar	Maui Creeper
Short-eared Owl	Iiwi
Black Noddy	Apapane

Haleakala is one of the nation's oldest national parks (established in 1916 as part of Hawaii National Park, later divided into Hawaii Volcanoes and Haleakala). It originally included only the upper part of the mountain, but was enlarged by the addition of Kipahulu Valley and the Seven Pools as a result of the efforts of The Nature Conservancy. The upper portion of Kipahulu Valley, where such rare birds as Akohekohe, Maui Parrotbill, and Nukupuu still exist, is a scientific reserve closed to the public. The drive up to the crater is spectacular with views of West Maui and the central valley. The road passes first through fields of sugar cane (look for Gray and Black francolins on the shoulder), then enters a mid-elevation ranching region of grassy pastures (all of this area was originally native koa forest!). The groves of trees among the pastures are mainly eucalyptus and are essentially birdless. The ranch lands are good places to look for Short-eared Owls, which are active by day, especially early morning and late afternoon. Eurasian Skylarks are numerous here and constantly fly up from the roadside ahead of an approaching car. Also look for Common Pheasants in the open fields. At mid-elevation, above and below the village of Kula, are numerous groves of Australian black-wattle acacia. The Red-billed Leiothrix is abundant in these thickets, but can be maddeningly difficult to see.

The best approach once you enter the national park is to drive directly to the summit area and work your way down. The crater tends to fill with clouds as day progresses, so the morning hours are more likely to produce a good view. Be sure to visit both the upper and lower lookouts; each has something of interest. The **Haleakala Summit** (10,023 ft.) is well above tree line in a barren, rocky alpine habitat. One of the few plants to grow in this area is the famous silversword, which looks something like a century plant but is actually a member of the sunflower family. Silverswords bloom in late summer. Between the alpine zone and the uppermost forests is a zone of native scrub comprising an impressive array of fascinating native plants. Among them are several relatives of the silversword (which look nothing like it but are genetically very similar), silver geranium, the red-flowering Haleakala sandalwood, pilo with its bright orange fruits, and yellow-flowered mamane. Native birds that can be seen in the scrub zone include Common Amakihi, Apapane, and Short-eared Owl but, to be honest, the plants are more interesting than the birds here! The alpine zone has even fewer birds, but is where the endangered Hawaiian Petrel nests (see species account). In both the alpine rocks and the scrub, look for coveys of Chukar. Haleakala is probably the most reliable place in Hawaii to find this introduced game bird. Be sure to check **Kalahaku Overlook** (a road to the right in the middle of a sharp curve as you descend from the summit). Not only is it a good place to see Chukar, but there is a display area for silverswords and a view of the crater from a different perspective. This is the best place to search for soaring White-tailed Tropicbirds, but you probably will not get a very close look.

The lower visitor center at **Park Headquarters** is well worth a visit. A few "park-tame" Nene (yes, they are "countable") sometimes hang around the buildings and lawns (see photo of unique park sign). These wild birds, which represent a reintroduced population, can be approached closely (but be careful not to harass them in any way). If none are present on the lawn between the parking lot and the visitor center, look among the service buildings out back. The geese are most often present in the fall and winter months. A few Northern Mockingbirds hang around this area as well.

No birder's visit to Haleakala National Park would be complete without a stop at **Hosmer Grove.** Just below the headquarters, a well-marked entrance road turns to the right opposite the private entrance to park staff residences. At the parking area is a small picnic/campground. When the mamane trees are in bloom, usually in spring and summer, the periphery of the picnic ground can be excellent birding. Hosmer Grove was planted early this century as an experiment to determine what trees from all over the world would be good for reforestation in Hawaii. Today, we wonder why they did not consider koa and ohia, but those were different times. All of the tall trees in the grove are alien species of eucalyptus, pine, acacia, and numerous others. Nevertheless, this is a good spot to find four native honeycreepers, including one Maui endemic. A loop trail begins at the bottom of the parking lot. It passes among tall eucalyptus and bends sharply to the right. At the bend, if you go straight ahead off the trail a few feet, you will come to the edge of a deep ravine in which several ohia trees grow. This is a good spot to look for Iiwi when the ohia trees are in bloom. Continuing around the trail you come to an open area surrounded by trees that provides a good vantage point to search the upper branches for Apapane. In the low bushes, look for Common Amakihi and listen for the sharp *tcherk* call note of the Maui Creeper. This endemic species is easy to overlook but is always present in Hosmer Grove. Further along the trail is an overlook into the ravine with a metal guard rail. This is an excellent place to pause and wait. All four honeycreepers can be seen as they forage in the trees below. (There has even been one report of Akohekohe here, but don't count on seeing one!) An interesting phenomenon to watch for is "trap-line feeding" by the Iiwi. These

birds set up a regular feeding path connecting good nectar sources and work it cyclically. If you get only a glimpse of your first Iiwi, just wait 15-20 minutes and the bird may well return to exactly the same spot. In early spring, when the mamane trees are in full bloom along the entrance road to the campground, Iiwi are common and conspicuous feeding among the yellow flowers.

The **Oheo Gulch** area of the park, popularly known as Seven Sacred Pools (a silly name made up by the tourist industry), is not as interesting for the birder as the summit area, but is worth the long drive for the waterfalls and beautiful lush valleys (see inset). An indispensable reference for this trip for anyone interested in natural history is *Maui's Hana Highway: a Visitor's Guide* by Angela Kay Kepler. The only bird of note along most of the way is the Hwa-mei (Melodious Laughing-thrush) which is heard more often than seen. From the lower part of the pools area, look for Black Noddies flying around the cliffs or over the ocean. Another good spot to see them is **Waianapanapa Caves State Park** just north of Hana.

Finally, so that you can impress your friends with your command of the Hawaiian language, a word about pronunciation. *Haleakala* means "house of the sun" (*hale* = house; *la* = sun), and *la* is one of those accented, long syllables. Thus the English translation has the same rhythm as the Hawaiian word: *HA-lay-a-ka-LAH*, the strongest accent on the last syllable. This is one of the most frequently mispronounced place names in Hawaii.

5. Waikamoi Preserve

Location: North slope of Haleakala, adjacent to the national park. Detail Map J.

Access: Entrance by special arrangement with The Nature Conservancy of Hawaii. Organized hikes for Conservancy members (you can join by sending a tax-deductible contribution of at least $10) depart from Hosmer Grove (see Site 3) on the second Sunday of each month. The National Park Service conducts bird walks into Waikamoi several times a week. For an up-to-date schedule, check with the park visitor center. To obtain a schedule of hikes or to make special arrangements for a private group to visit the preserve, write to Preserve Manager, Waikamoi Preserve, P. O. Box 1716, Makawao, HI 96768-1716 or phone (808) 572-7849.

Precautions: Do not attempt to enter the preserve on your own. Not only will you be guilty of trespassing, but you will almost certainly get lost in the maze of confusingly flagged trails. The Nature Conservancy is very cooperative in arranging for visits, and in any case you are very unlikely to find the rare birds unless accompanied by someone who knows exactly where to go. You will probably have to join an organized group because the Conservancy does not have staff available to guide individuals. Trails in the preserve are "unimproved," steep, and muddy. Expect to get wet and dirty. Alien plants and animals constitute one of the greatest threats to native ecosystems in Hawaii. Check your boots before hiking into Waikamoi to make sure you are not tracking in foreign mud or seeds.

Notable Species:	Red-billed Leiothrix	Iiwi
	Maui Parrotbill	Akohekohe (Crested Honeycreeper)
	Common Amakihi	Apapane
	Maui Creeper	

Waikamoi Preserve was established in 1983 by The Nature Conservancy of Hawaii as part of its Endangered Hawaiian Forest Bird Project. It preserves a dagger of land north of Haleakala National Park that previously had no protection. Much of the most accessible part of the preserve is given over to a huge plantation of alien trees, part of Hosmer Grove (Site 3). Birds in this area are the same as those listed for that part of the grove that lies within the national park. To see the rare Akohekohe or the very rare Maui Parrotbill, one formerly had to hike deep into the preserve beyond the planted forest. Recently, however, both of these species have been turning up in more accessible places within the preserve (see the respective species accounts). Both are occasionally observed on regularly scheduled bird walks (but don't hold your breath for a parrotbill). The best areas for the rarities require the services of an experienced guide. Waikamoi Preserve is a shining example of the outstanding conservation work conducted by The Nature Conservancy of Hawaii. For further information about the Conservancy's activities, write to TNCH, 1116 Smith St., Suite 201, Honolulu, HI 96817.

6. Waikamoi Flume
(Contributed by J. William Eley)

Location: North slope of Haleakala, east of Olinda and north of the Waikamoi Preserve. Detail Map J.

Access: Entrance by permission of Haleakala Ranch, whose property you must cross to reach the flume. You must sign a waiver form, which absolves the ranch of any blame should you injure yourself while on ranch land or beyond, at the ranch headquarters. To reach the headquarters from Kahului, take Haleakala Highway and turn left on Highway 377 towards the National Park and the Crater (prominently marked) just above

Pukalani. Approximately a mile up Highway 377 look for a polo field on the left, and a small road to the left just past the field. Turn left and continue 0.3 mi to the next intersection and turn left again. Haleakala Ranch headquarters, a gray house with several large mailboxes out front, is 0.2 mi further on the right. Tell whomever answers your knock on the door that you wish to sign the waiver form to cross ranch lands to go birding in the state forest area. You may obtain permission a couple of days in advance of your hike if you like.

To reach the trailhead, retrace your path to the first intersection and turn left (a right turn takes you back to Highway 377). Proceed to Olinda Rd, turn right, and continue several miles to a gate at the end of the road. Park well off the road and do not block any driveways. Begin your hike by crossing through the opening in the gate at the end of the road. At about a quarter mile, follow the road left at the first major intersection. Continue up the road through open fields (a good place to see Skylarks) for about a quarter mile into a grove of eucalyptus trees and through another gate (you may have to climb over). The road leaves the grove and traverses another field before entering **Makawao State Forest**. After about a mile, you enter the **Koolau State Forest** (you may have to climb another gate here). The road continues less than three miles to two large concrete ponds. Go left around the left pond and a short distance up a hill to a small open building. To the left are a rain gauge and weather station which flank the

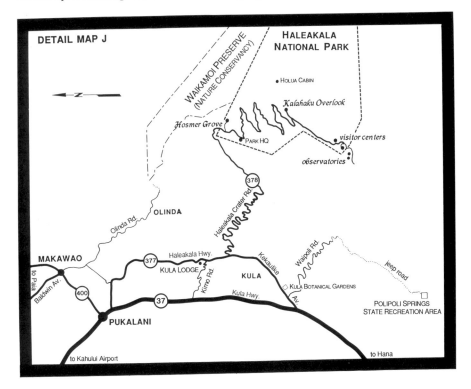

beginning of the flume trail. A sturdy boardwalk that makes hiking easy follows the flume for several miles. This route has been used by pig hunters for years, but you will likely find it deserted.

Precautions: Do not attempt to enter this area without authorization. The ranch is very cooperative in granting permission as long as you sign the waiver form (which you should have with you on the hike). Be aware that the East Maui Irrigation Company often works with heavy equipment along the road in the state forest to maintain its irrigation systems. Be prepared to give way to trucks and equipment along the road. The boardwalk is very narrow with some sections spanning drop-offs of almost 100 feet. Hike with caution! Remember before continuing too far that you have a long hike back to your car.

Notable Species: Red-billed Leiothrix
Common Amakihi
Maui Creeper
Apapane
Akohekohe (Crested Honeycreeper)
Iiwi

The beginning of this portion of the hike is through an area much like Hosmer Grove (Maui 4), with such alien trees as eucalyptus, pine, and acacia, but the introduced vegetation is soon replaced by native koa-ohia forest. The beautiful forest in the flume area represents the lower portions of the Waikamoi Preserve forest. Four honeycreepers (Amakihi, Iiwi, Apapane, and Maui Creeper) are common, and the Akohekohe has also been seen here. This locality has been little studied by birders or ornithologists, so no one knows what other rarities may be present. Although the area is remote, the flume boardwalk probably provides the easiest stroll through pristine native forest in all of Hawaii.

7. East Maui Wilderness

Location: Northeast slope of Haleakala above 4,000 feet.

Access: Restricted and logistically very difficult. The wilderness area can be reached on foot only by a long hike across Haleakala Crater. Permits for overnight camping in the park can be obtained from The Superintendent, Haleakala National Park, P. O. Box 369, Makawao, HI 96768. Although the best areas for birds lie outside the park, you will have to camp in the park because the heart of the wilderness area is now a state natural area reserve where camping is not permitted. It is physically possible but legally difficult to get into the area by helicopter. You have to land in the park, for which special permission must be obtained. No commercial chopper pilot would risk his license by landing without proper clearance. Because this area is very sensitive to disturbance, use of helicopters is kept to the bare minimum necessary to conduct scientific surveillance.

Precautions: An expedition into the wilderness of East Maui is a major undertaking recommended only for experienced hikers in excellent physical condition. It requires a one-way trek of about fifteen miles at very high elevation (the crater floor is around 8,000 feet, and you must hike over the rim on the far side and drop down to the upper edge of the forest at about 7,000 feet). You must carry your own water for the crater crossing. If you plan to stay several days in the wilderness, you may be able to use rain water, but that is unpredictable. Stream water even deep in the forest must be boiled or treated chemically before use because of the presence of feral pigs. Be sure not to add to the birds' problems by tracking in alien weed seeds.

Notable Species: Bishop's Oo   Akepa
Maui Parrotbill   Akohekohe (Crested Honeycreeper)
Nukupuu   Poo-uli
Maui Creeper

The above "wish list" is included for completeness rather than to imply that one could actually see all of these rare birds. Even most researchers who have spent considerable time in the Upper Hanawi watershed, where the Poo-uli was discovered in 1973, have not seen all of them. The most challenging ones are Bishop's Oo (seen by perhaps no more than three living persons) and Nukupuu, which remains one of the author's nemeses. The Poo-uli can be seen only if one knows exactly where to look; the tiny remaining population is very localized. Without the guidance of someone familiar with the area, a quest for this bird and other rarities is nearly hopeless. These birds' existence is very precarious. Efforts are being made to fence out feral pigs from the last stronghold of the Poo-uli, but it is a race against time. Pigs have already trashed the place where the species was first found and are inexorably closing in on the last unspoiled area. Because the Poo-uli is a bird of the undergrowth, it appears particularly sensitive to such disturbance. The intrepid birder determined to try for this bird might consider volunteering for work on fencing or survey projects conducted on an irregular basis by the State of Hawaii. For information about these projects, write to the Division of Forestry and Wildlife, 1151 Punchbowl St., Honolulu, HI 96813.

8. Polipoli Springs

Location: Western slope of Haleakala in Maui upcountry above Kula.

Access: Open to the public. To reach Polipoli Springs, follow directions for Haleakala Crater (Site 4), but do not take the second left turn onto Crater Road and continue ahead on Rt. 377 through Kula. Watch for Kula Botanical Gardens on the left. Turn left onto Waipoli Road just past the gardens. Waipoli Road ends after about ten miles at Polipoli. Camping permits must be obtained in advance. A rustic but comfortable and reasonably priced cabin that can sleep up to ten is also available by advance reservation. For both of these, write to the Division of State Parks, P. O. Box 1049, Wailuku, HI 96793 or telephone (808) 244-4354.

Precautions: Only the first part of Waipoli Road is paved; the second part can be very rough and muddy, but four-wheel-drive is not usually necessary if you drive slowly and carefully.

Notable Species:	Common Pheasant	**Common Amakihi**
	Short-eared Owl	**Maui Creeper**
	Eurasian Skylark	**Apapane**
	Red-billed Leiothrix	

Polipoli Springs State Recreation Area comprises a planted forest of eucalyptus and foreign conifers similar to Hosmer Grove (Site 3). Surprisingly, the three honeycreepers listed are quite common, particularly the Maui Creeper. If you like to get away from it all, Polipoli is for you. On the way, you might want to stop at **Kula Botanical Gardens** (admission $2.50; open daily 9 am - 4 pm), a beautiful exhibit of both native and foreign plants. The gardens are one of the best places to get a good look at a Red-billed Leiothrix.

9. Molokini Islet

Location: Off the southwest corner of East Maui, between Maui and Kahoolawe.

Access: Numerous party boats out of Lahaina, Maalaea Harbor, and Kihei visit Molokini for snorkeling and diving. Landing on the island is not permitted.

Notable Species: Bulwer's Petrel
                         Wedge-tailed Shearwater

Molokini, a crescent-shaped flooded cinder cone, is one of the finest snorkeling spots in Hawaii. The island itself is steep-sided and undercut so that landing is very difficult as well as illegal. Wedge-tailed Shearwaters nest in burrows in the inner wall of the crater and can be easily seen from anchored snorkeling boats. The birds dive out of their burrows very quickly and often fly close by the boats. They are active here all day, so can be seen during the midday hours when most of the organized excursions are in the crater. Bulwer's Petrels also nest on the islet, but are more likely to be seen at dusk than at midday. The trip out to Molokini provides an excellent opportunity, between December and May, to see humpback whales. Unfortunately, the channels between Lanai, Kahoolawe, and Maui are too shallow to attract many pelagic seabirds, and the trip can seem almost birdless. During the spring months, a few Sooty Shearwaters and White-tailed Tropicbirds may be seen in addition to the Wedge-tails. Boats to Molokini are numerous and varied in their offerings. Most hotels have a display with brochures describing what is available. Most Molokini boats depart from Maalaea Harbor, on the south side of the Maui isthmus, and Kihei. Formerly, a few Molokini boats operated out of Lahaina, so inquire locally if that is more convenient for you. Lahaina is not of much birding interest although it is the best place on Maui to find Red-crested Cardinals (look for them around the big banyan tree on Front Street). It was the old capital of the Kingdom of Hawaii and a major stopover port for whalers. Lahaina retains much of its unique character despite a plethora of T-shirt and souvenir shops, and is well worth a visit. An exhibit of native Hawaiian plants, including many species of hibiscus, is located adjacent to the main dock behind the banyan tree.

Pronunciation note: "Maalaea" is a five-syllable word, accented on the first and fourth, *Mah-ah-lah-AY-ah*. However, most of the boat operators and tourist industry ignoramuses will not understand you if you say it correctly. They call it *Mah-LYE-ah*, as if it were spelled "Malaia."

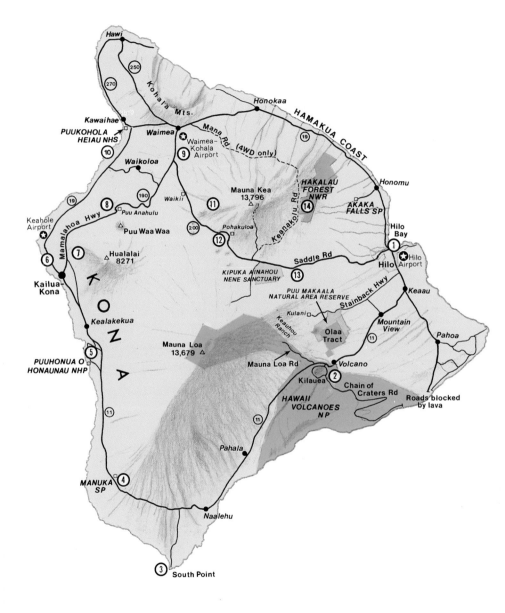

Hawaii

THE BIG ISLAND (HAWAII)

The Island of Hawaii, slightly smaller than Jamaica, is more than twice the size of all the other Hawaiian Islands combined. To avoid confusing the island with the State of Hawaii, local residents almost universally refer to it as the Big Island. Geologically the youngest in the archipelago, the Big Island is also the only one with currently active volcanoes. As a result, its landforms and landscapes are unique in Hawaii. The island as we see it today was formed by five separate volcanoes. Kohala Mountain at the northern tip is the oldest and, at least on the windward side, more closely resembles the eroded landforms of the other islands. Mauna Kea ("White Mountain"), at 13,796 feet the highest peak in the Hawaiian Islands, can also be considered the world's tallest mountain because it rises from the sea floor 18,000 feet below the surface. Mauna Kea is dormant and exhibits the characteristic cinder-cone-pocked summit of a senile volcano. The other three volcanoes have all erupted in historic times, although Hualalai (8,271 feet) in North Kona is now dormant. Mauna Loa ("Long Mountain"), at 13,677 feet, is nearly as high as Mauna Kea, but has a quite different smooth domed profile. Both high peaks may be snow-capped during winter months but snow persists much longer on Mauna Kea. The other volcano is Kilauea, which is peculiar in that it does not form a peak of its own (those who refer to it as "Mt. Kilauea" have obviously never been there). Because Kilauea's caldera is in a "shelf" on the flank of Mauna Loa, its lavas always flow downhill in more or less the same direction, so no cone builds up. Nevertheless, Kilauea and Mauna Loa are separate lava systems. Lava flows of all ages are an ever-present aspect of Big Island landscapes.

As might be expected, the windward (eastern) slopes of Mauna Kea and Mauna Loa receive heavy rainfall as a result of the northeast tradewinds. However, both mountains are so high that the trades are almost completely blocked from the leeward slopes. The "saddle" between the two mountains is relatively dry, even desertlike in places. However, the western slopes of Hualalai and Mauna Loa, comprising the region called Kona, also have a rainforest belt which results from a distinctive locally generated weather system (not to be confused with "kona weather"). A typical daily cycle begins with a clear morning, then, as the sun rises high enough to heat the Kona slopes, an updraft is created that brings moisture-laden cooler air in from the sea. As this air rises, clouds form and by midday the mountaintops are obscured. It is this midday cloud cover that favors the cultivation of Kona coffee. Rain often falls in late afternoon on the mountain slopes, but as the land cools at night the air flow is reversed and the clouds drift out to sea to begin the cycle anew the following day. Birders in Kona should keep this usually predictable pattern in mind. The Big Island also has true rain shadow areas that are very dry. Savannah-like grasslands dominate the districts of South Kohala and North Kona and the South Point area.

Hawaii, with the islands' only crow, hawk, and goose as well as many kinds of Hawaiian honeycreepers, originally had the lion's share of endemic bird species among the islands. In general, its endangered species are less critically imperiled than those of other islands because they enjoy much more extensive tracts of high-elevation habitat. Only two Big Island birds (Ou and Hawaiian Crow) are in the "nearly hopeless" category for the birder. Despite this fact, seeing native birds takes some effort and ingenuity. Most of the best habitat is in roadless areas or on tracts of private and government land closed to the public. Also, no one locality will produce all species; one must visit a number of widely scattered habitats. The Big Island has also been "favored" as a release site for introduced birds, especially around Puu Waa Waa Ranch in North Kona (see Detail Map O). Not only was the ranch the center of state efforts to introduce game birds but also the ranch owners at one time were aviculturists active in the Hui Manu and released numerous kinds of finches and waxbills. These species have now spread widely but Puu Waa Waa (see Site 8) remains the heart of the range for most of them.

Tourism, while important, assumes a less prominent economic position on the Big Island than elsewhere in Hawaii. Ranching and agriculture dominate the economies of most towns. Most resorts are along the Kona Coast. Hilo, the island's largest city, has relatively few hotels. Waimea, center of the Parker Ranch, has several modest but adequate motels well located for birding. Also popular with birders is the century-old Volcano House (see Site 2) on the rim of Kilauea Crater. The Big Island is served by three major airports: Hilo International, Keahole in Kona, and Waimea-Kohala in Waimea. Rental cars are available in both Hilo and Kona, and may be dropped off (for a fee, of course) at the other airport. Four-wheel-drive vehicles can be rented in Hilo and Kona.

Common and Widespread Birds

> Common Pheasant
> Pacific Golden-Plover*
> Wandering Tattler*
> Ruddy Turnstone*
> Sanderling*
> Rock Dove
> Spotted Dove
> Zebra Dove
> Eurasian Skylark
> Common Myna
> Japanese White-eye
> Northern Cardinal
> House Finch
> Common Amakihi
> Apapane
> House Sparrow
> Nutmeg Mannikin
> *seasonal

1. Hilo Ponds

Location: In Hilo near the airport. Detail Map K.

Access: Both ponds are easily accessible on public streets. **Loko Waka Pond** (sometimes spelled Lokoaka or Lokoaku on maps) is on Kalanianaole St. (Rt. 19) east of the industrial port facilities. From the airport, turn right on Kanoelehua Ave. (Rt. 11), then right again at the next traffic light. Bear left at the Y for Kalanianaole Street. The pond is on the right about three miles from the intersection and directly across the highway from a public park on a small scenic bay. **Waiakea Pond** is surrounded by Wailoa River State Recreation Area and can be approached in a variety of ways. A good place for viewing is located at the end of Piilani Street, which intersects with Rt. 11 near the airport. Piilani can also be reached via Manono Street between Kamehameha Avenue and E. Lanikaula Street. A second access point where you can see a part of the pond not visible from the previous viewing area is on Kilauea Avenue where it crosses the Wailoa River (which here is a channelized concrete canal). Look for a huge banyan tree that shades the viewing area.

Precautions: Traffic on Kalanianaole Avenue is heavy and everyone seems to be in a hurry. Do not stand in the roadway while viewing the pond.

Notable Species Cattle Egret
         Black-crowned Night-Heron
         Northern Pintail
         Northern Shoveler
         Ring-necked Duck
         Lesser Scaup
         Hawaiian Coot

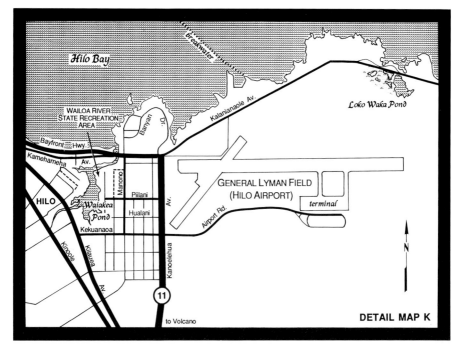

DETAIL MAP K

Despite their proximity to human activities, these two ponds have produced a surprising list of rare birds over the years and should always be checked if you are in the area. Cattle Egrets used to maintain a huge rookery in trees at Loko Waka Pond, but because they were a hazard to aircraft at the nearby airport, control measures were taken and their numbers greatly reduced. None of the migratory ducks listed above are always present, but all are fairly regular visitors. Other species that have turned up on these ponds include Green-backed Heron, Great Blue Heron, Pied-billed Grebe, Tufted Duck, Redhead, Canada ("Cackling") Goose, and even Snow Goose. Be sure to check the small backwater of Waiakea Pond off Kilauea Avenue. It is an inauspicious-looking spot, recently overgrown with rank vegetation, but is a traditional loafing spot for ducks. Many ornamental waterfowl (mostly Mallards and Muscovy Ducks) are kept at Waiakea and, to a lesser extent, at Loko Waka; wild birds often "take up" with them and act just as tame.

2. Hawaii Volcanoes National Park

Location: Southern part of the Big Island, encompassing the summit of Mauna Loa, Kilauea Crater, and a large portion of the island's south coast. Detail Map L.

Access: The park entrance is just off Rt. 11 about one mile west of the town of Volcano and is well marked with signs. Entrance fees are charged (Golden Eagle and Golden Age passes accepted). A former entrance near the coast is now blocked by recent lava flows. The "Mauna Loa Strip" can be visited without paying the entrance fee (take Mauna Loa Road mauka from Rt. 11 about a mile west of the main park entrance). The Kilauea Crater area can be toured by taking the circular Crater Rim Drive in either direction. To reach the coast in the park, take Chain of Craters Road (well marked) off Crater Rim Drive. You must return via the same route (about 45 minutes one way).

Precautions: Sulphurous fumes from Halemaumau and other craters in the park may be hazardous to persons with respiratory problems. Always wipe your binoculars after being in such areas to prevent formation of damaging acid. Heed all warning signs in the park and stay on trails. Sharp aa lava can produce very serious cuts if you fall. Carry extra drinking water when you make the trip down Chain of Craters Road.

Notable Species:	White-tailed Tropicbird	Black Noddy
	Nene (Hawaiian Goose)	Elepaio
	Hawaiian Hawk	Omao
	Chukar	Melodious Laughing-thrush
	Kalij Pheasant	**Red-billed Leiothrix**
	Common Pheasant (green form)	Iiwi
	California Quail	**Apapane**

Hawaii Volcanoes National Park, established in 1916 to preserve the two active volcanoes, actually comprises a wide variety of scenic wonders and habitats. Just inside the entrance booth on the right is the **Park Visitor Center** (open 9-4 daily) which features exhibits, movies and videos about recent eruptions, and a shop with books and maps. Across the road from the visitor center is the **Volcano House**, a hotel that has been in existence, in several different buildings, for over a century. It has a pricey restaurant best visited at breakfast and dinner; it is an unbelievable mob scene at midday when the Kona-Hilo tour buses stop to feed and water their herds. Volcano House is small, so make reservations well in advance (Box 53, Hawaii Volcanoes National Park, HI 96718; 967-7321). Just outside the park, recently opened **Kilauea Lodge** (P. O. Box 116, Volcano, HI 96785; 967-7366) provides an alternative. It has rustic rooms and an excellent restaurant. These two are the only modern hotels in Hawaii where you can be awakened by the songs of Omao and Apapane.

　　Crater Rim Drive circles the main crater of Kilauea Volcano. These directions are given counterclockwise, but the drive can be approached equally well the other way. As you leave the visitor center heading west you will note an abrupt change in the vegetation that represents the shift from the windward to the leeward slope in this part of the island. Much more rain falls on the windward side. As you proceed you will pass an eyesore on the right known as Kilauea Military Camp, an "R and R" facility that, unfortunately, antedates the park. Further around the drive you will come to the **Volcano Observatory and Jaggar Museum** on the left. The museum is excellent, and the overlook will provide your first close look at Halemaumau (see photo), a deep pit in the middle of the crater. Look closely and you will probably see White-tailed

Tropicbirds circling in the fumes. The museum sells a U. S. Geological Survey Map of the park and vicinity that is excellent for birders because it includes some areas along the Saddle Road that are not accurately shown on most maps. Around the observatory parking lot, look for Chukars and Hawaiian Hawks, both of which are seen here from time to time. You can get a closer look at the tropicbirds by continuing around the loop to a parking area from which you can walk to the edge of Halemaumau. From this point on around the loop until you enter forest, watch for Nene. They are naturally tame and may be sitting right by the road. A particularly good place for them is around **Keanakakoi Crater** where there is a place to park and spend some time looking. Continuing the loop you will pass the turn-off for Chain of Craters Road (discussed below), and a left turn into a parking lot for a boardwalk called **Devastation Trail**. The trail is more interesting geologically than ornithologically, but is a good place to see Apapane and Common Amakihi and to hear Omao (they're easier to see elsewhere). The next attraction on the loop is **Thurston**

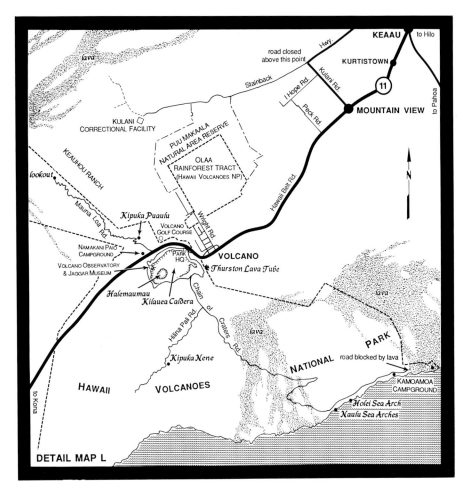

DETAIL MAP L

Lava Tube, a must-see for any park visitor and a good spot for birds. Mornings before 10 and afternoons after 4 are the best times to visit to avoid a steady stream of jaded tourists. At the entrance to the lava tube is a balconylike lookout where one can look directly into the tops of tall ohia trees. Omao are easier to see here than almost any other accessible locality. Other species include abundant Apapane (surprisingly ignored in the display near the entrance) and a few Elepaio. Ou, which were seen near here in the 1950s, are no longer present. Continuing on Crater Rim Drive from the lava tube will return you to the park entrance booth.

Chain of Craters Road is a spectacular drive from Kilauea Crater to the site of the most recent lava flows on the coast. The road is steep but very well engineered and a joy to drive. Watch for Hawaiian Hawks as you descend. Hilina Pali Road which leads off to the right will take you to a campground at Kipuka Nene. The birds for which the spot is named are supposedly present, but in recent visits I did not find them. Recently, Red-billed Francolins *Francolinus adspersus*, not yet admitted to the official Hawaii list, have been seen in this area. When you reach the coast, look for parking areas on the right from which you can walk to the edge of the cliffs. Holei Sea Arch (see photo) is an especially good spot to stop. Black Noddies nest in the cliffs and can be easily seen going and coming all year long. The Wahaula Visitor Center that used to be just beyond this point fell victim to a lava flow in 1989, and the road now dead-ends.

Another "wing" of the park that is excellent for birding is the **Mauna Loa Strip.** Mauna Loa Road climbs the volcano for ten miles to a dead end at just under 7,000 feet. A short distance from the main highway is **Kipuka Puaulu**, popularly called Bird Park. A lovely and easy hiking trail makes a loop through the kipuka, which, despite its name, is more interesting for its plants than for its birds. It is, however, an excellent place to find Kalij Pheasants that can often be approached quite closely if you are quiet. Listen for rustling in the leaves as a way of finding Melodious Laughing-thrushes which, even when close, are hard to see. At least one pair of Hawaiian Hawks have nested in this vicinity in recent years. Just above Kipuka Puaulu is Kipuka Ki, another good place to stop and walk along the road. Elepaio, Omao, and Red-billed Leiothrix are common here, and Akiapolaau have been reported but cannot be expected. Kalij Pheasants may be on the road as you ascend, and California Quail often sit on the pavement late in the day to take advantage of the radiated warmth. The upper part of Mauna Loa Road (above a cattle guard and powerline crossing) is the best place in the national park to find Iiwi. The best way to find them is to "stake out" a blooming ohia tree and just wait. Nene used to be seen regularly at the upper terminus of the road, but not lately.

A nearby locality that is adjacent to but not in the national park is the **Volcano Golf Course.** It is on a short mauka spur off Rt. 11 between Mauna Loa Road and the main park entrance. Nene sometimes loaf on the golf course in the late afternoon, but

are not as frequently seen now as formerly, probably because of increased helicopter traffic (you can take a chopper from here to view eruptions in remote areas). "Green" Pheasants, formerly classed as a separate species but now regarded as a form of Common Pheasant, are also often seen on the golf course.

3. South Point

Location: Southernmost extremity of the Island of Hawaii.

Access: South Point Road leads makai off Rt. 11 (Hawaii Belt Road or Mamalahoa Highway) about six miles west of Naalehu. The ten-mile spur is narrow but paved. Some (but not all) rental car companies restrict driving on this road. At the southern end of the road, look for a stone wall that encloses a portion of the point area. Drive to the left of this wall (off the pavement) until you come to a break in it. You may not drive through the opening, but it is a convenient place to park.

Precautions: South Point Road is perfectly safe if you take it slow but be cautious when meeting other vehicles; the pavement is not wide enough for two and one must yield.

Notable Species	Wedge-tailed Shearwater	Sanderling
	Brown Booby	Black Noddy
	Bristle-thighed Curlew	Short-eared Owl
	Ruddy Turnstone	Rock Dove

Ka Lae, or South Point as it is more widely known, is the southernmost point in the United States of America. It lies at the tip of a barren, wind-swept peninsula but its sheer desolation has a certain appeal and it is a popular place to visit. The upper portion of the access road passes through ranch lands and close by a "wind farm" that generates electricity. Short-eared Owls hunt over the pastures and fields throughout the length of the road. The point itself is a good place to watch for seabirds offshore. A spotting scope is very helpful. At some seasons Wedge-tailed Shearwaters and Black Noddies congregate by the thousands off the point. At other times, the ocean may appear birdless here. The timing and seasonality of seabirds is not well known in this area, so no one knows the best times to visit South Point. The grassy area on the eastern side of the point is excellent for skylarks and upland shorebirds such as turnstones and golden-plovers, and tattlers are common on the rocks around the point. Bristle-thighed Curlews have been seen here in April, but are far from regular. They should be looked for in the fall as well. The Rock Doves at South Point are probably as truly wild as any feral pigeons anywhere.

4. Manuka State Park

Location: On Rt. 11 (Hawaii Belt Road) in South Kona Forest Reserve.

Access: From Kona, drive south until you pass the "world's largest macadamia nut orchard" and enter the forest reserve. Look for the park on the left. From Volcano, look for the park on the right after you pass Ocean View Estates subdivision.

Notable Species: Elepaio
                          Common Amakihi
                          Apapane

       This small roadside park is a real gem. Its most important attraction is a labelled collection of native and exotic trees and shrubs that includes several endangered species nearly extinct in the wild. The most impressive collection is of native hibiscus. The species listed above are easy to see in the park. When in bloom, a white-flowered variety of the wiliwili tree adjacent to the picnic shelter is often full of Common Amakihi that can be studied closely. Of course, it also attracts the ubiquitous Japanese White-eye.

5. Kealakekua Bay and Honaunau

Location: In South Kona, on a makai loop off Rt. 11 (Hawaii Belt Road) just south of Kealakekua and Captain Cook. Detail Map M.

Access: From the north, take Napoopoo Road which angles to the right off Rt. 11 in the village of Captain Cook. This descends steeply to Kealakekua Bay and Napoopoo Beach Park. From there, take the paved but narrow and rough coastal road south to Puuhonua o Honaunau National Historical Park. The park charges an entrance fee (Golden Eagle and Golden Age passes accepted). Return to Rt. 11 via Rt. 160, a much better road. From the south, take Rt. 160 which branches to the left off Rt. 11 in the village of Keokea and follow the directions in reverse.

Notable Species: **Hawaiian Hawk**   **Yellow-billed Cardinal**
                              Wandering Tattler   Lavender Waxbill

      This is an area of great cultural and historical significance that almost any visitor to Hawaii will want to experience. The **Puuhonua o Honaunau National Historical Park**, formerly and still popularly known as City of Refuge, presents an excellent interpretive exhibit about life in pre-European Hawaii. It preserves the remains of a *pu'uhonua*, a place of "refuge" that was the ancient equivalent of a prison. *Kapu* (taboo) breakers who could reach the *pu'uhonua* at least escaped certain death, and after a period of penance and performance of the proper ceremonies could, in some cases, return to society. At nearby **Kealakekua Bay** you will find a particularly well-preserved *heiau*, a pre-Christian stone temple. Across the bay is a white monolith erected in honor of Captain James Cook, who died at that spot in an unfortunate misunderstanding with the previously friendly Hawaiians whom he had recently

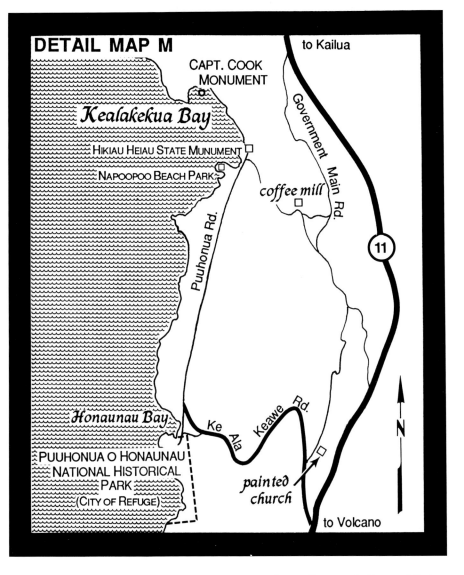

DETAIL MAP M

to Kailua

CAPT. COOK
MONUMENT

Kealakekua Bay

HIKIAU HEIAU STATE MUNUMENT

NAPOOPOO BEACH PARK

coffee mill

Government Main Rd.

Puuhonua Rd.

11

Honaunau Bay

Ke Ala Keawe Rd.

PUUHONUA O HONAUNAU
NATIONAL HISTORICAL
PARK
(CITY OF REFUGE)

painted church

N

to Volcano

"discovered." Today, the bay is a marine preserve with excellent snorkeling and diving. **Napoopoo Beach** near the *heiau* is small but popular. Behind the beach is a small wet area, not much more than a puddle, that should be checked for rare shorebirds. A Spotted Sandpiper once spent the winter here. This area in general is not especially "birdy," but Yellow-billed Cardinals are abundant and several estrildid finches have been reported including Lavender Waxbill (look for them around the private homes adjacent to the parking lot at the national park). On the slopes between the main highway and the coast, watch for Hawaiian Hawks. At dusk during winter months, plovers, turnstones, and tattlers gather by the hundreds to roost on exposed lava on the makai side of the reconstructed temple house at the national historical park. An added treat if you are there at that time of day (as if the impressive Kona sunset is not enough) is the presence of hoary bats (Hawaii's only native land mammal) hawking insects overhead.

6. Aimakapa Pond

Location: North Kona District of the Big Island between Keahole Airport and Kailua-Kona. Detail Map N.

Access: Access is unrestricted, but entry at present is "at your own risk." From Kailua, drive north on Rt. 19 toward the airport. Look for a sign and a road to the left leading to Honokohau Boat Harbor. Follow the entrance road and take the first right turn into the boat storage area. Follow this road all the way around until the pavement ends. Park here. Cross over the stone wall to the right (unless they have been removed, the letters N. B. and an arrow painted in the roadway point toward the correct trail). Even without the graffiti, the cross-over points are obvious. Follow the trail across the lava flow until it enters a grove of kiawe trees. Bear to the right when the trail forks and follow it until you see an opening to the beach. Walk out to the water's edge and bear right. Eventually, the wall of vegetation behind the sand opens up and you can cross over the dune to see the pond. One portion of the pond can be seen only from an access point through the bushes further around in the same direction along the beach.

Precautions: Do not leave valuables visible in your parked car at the boat harbor. The letters "N. B." stand for "nude beach," and so it is. You may create something of a stir among the bathers as you approach with your binoculars and spotting scopes but, frankly, it is their problem, not yours. Just go about your business as if everything were perfectly normal and no one will bother you.

Notable Species:

Pied-billed Grebe	American Wigeon
Cattle Egret	Gray Francolin
Black-crowned Night-Heron	**Hawaiian Coot**
Mallard	**Hawaiian Stilt**
Northern Pintail	**Yellow-billed Cardinal**
Blue-winged Teal	Saffron Finch
Northern Shoveler	Warbling Silverbill

The name of this ancient fishpond has an irregular accent on the last syllable and thus is pronounced *EYE-mah-kah-PAH* , not "I'm a coppa." It is included in the recently established and as yet undeveloped **Kaloko-Honokohau National Historical Park**. Because so few ponds survive in a relatively natural state in Kona, Aimakapa is a wonderful "migrant trap" where many rare and unexpected species have turned up over the years. Birds come and go fairly frequently, especially in spring and fall, so if you

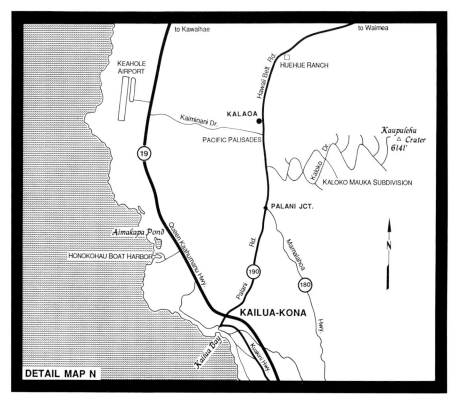

have the time it is worth checking the pond daily while you are in the area. Aimakapa Pond is the only nesting locality in the Hawaiian Islands for both Pied-billed Grebe and Blue-winged Teal. The teal have nested here only irregularly, but the grebe colony is thriving. The grebes, long regarded as only casual visitors to the Hawaiian Islands, began nesting here in the early 1980s. They represent the only certain natural colonization of the islands by a mainland species in historic times. Two endangered species, Hawaiian Coot and (Hawaiian) Black-necked Stilt, nest here also. Wintering ducks are sometimes present in the hundreds and almost always include a few unusual species among the more common ones. Garganey, Eurasian Wigeon, Tufted Duck, and Gadwall have been found recently. No one knows for sure the origin of the Mallards that are often present, but more or less by mutual agreement, birders in Hawaii regard them as "countable." This locality is also excellent for shorebirds. Do not neglect the wave-washed lava flow along the beach on the way in. Such rarities as Siberian (Gray-tailed) Tattler and Rufous-necked Stint have been found on the lava recently. In the kiawe grove along the trail to the pond, Yellow-billed Cardinals are abundant and easy to see. In the scrubby vegetation on the open lava flow, look for the cardinals as well as Saffron Finches and Warbling Silverbills. Aimakapa Pond is one of Hawaii's most important and accessible birding localities. Don't miss it.

7. Kaloko Mauka Subdivision

Location: West slope of Hualalai above Kailua-Kona. Detail Map N.

Access: Public highway. From Kailua, take Mamalahoa Hwy. (Rt. 190) mauka toward Waimea. Four miles from town you will pass the intersection with Rt. 180 (Palani Jct.)

From this point, begin looking for Kaloko Drive where you should turn right. The street-name sign is set quite far back and is only visible at the last minute, so drive slowly. Kaloko Drive zigzags steeply mauka. Side streets either dead-end or loop back into Kaloko. The main road eventually ends at a ranch gate. Just before the gate, a spur to the left ascends steeply to a water tank, the highest point you can reach by car, where you can park and turn around.

Precautions: Although the road is wide and well-paved, it is quite steep in places. Remember to use lower gears when you descend to avoid overheating your brakes. Do your birding from the roadway (the shoulders are wide) and respect private property.

Notable Species:	**Hawaiian Hawk**	**Yellow-fronted Canary**
	Kalij Pheasant	Common Amakihi
	Wild Turkey	**Iiwi**
	Saffron Finch	Apapane

When this subdivision was first established in the late 1970s it was one of Hawaii's best birding sites. The road penetrated an almost pristine montane native forest. From the paved highway one could see such rarities as Akepa and Hawaiian Crow. However, as human usage increased in the area, the habitat deteriorated rapidly. Cutting of hapuu (tree-ferns) opened up the undergrowth, and feral pigs exacerbated the damage. Lot owners seemed to prefer to cut the trees down rather than enjoy them. The crows are gone along with several other species (Akepa, Hawaii Creeper, Elepaio) and introduced birds and plants are increasingly in evidence. Even so, though this is no longer a prime birding spot, it is a readily accessible locality where at least a few native birds, including Iiwi, can be seen easily. At least one pair of Hawaiian Hawks has nested in the area recently, and some patches of forest are still beautiful. Look for the garlands of ieie (a climbing relative of pandanus) in the ohia trees. At times, ieie looks like clumps of bromeliads, but is not related to them. The red fruiting bodies, which were a favorite food of the Hawaiian Crow, are clustered at the ends of the stems. An aviculturist on one of the side streets may be responsible for the escaped parrots that are being seen with increasing frequency in the Kailua area.

8. Puu Anahulu

Location: In North Kona, about nineteen miles from Kailua on Mamalahoa Highway, near Puu Waa Waa cinder cone. Detail Map O.

Access: The area is traversed by Mamalahoa Highway (Rt. 190, Hawaii Belt Road) and can be reached easily from either Waimea or Kailua. From Kailua, take Rt. 190 toward Waimea. After you pass Huehue Ranch, the highway passes through an undeveloped area of lava flows and dry scrub. Soon the fluted cinder cone of Puu Waa Waa will be visible mauka. The road is fairly straight until you reach the entrance to Puu Waa Waa Ranch (just below the cinder cone), where it turns sharply left and climbs the side of an obvious steep hill. Look for a wide pullout on the makai side of the road where you can safely park. You can look out from the road into the tops of trees and down into the grassy flats below. Another safe place to park is on the mauka side just beyond where the road leaves the steep hill. Continuing in the same direction, look for the entrance to Puu Lani Ranch, a new luxury subdivision, on the right. As of this writing, the area is open to the public, but a control gate at the entrance to insure privacy of the residents is planned. When construction is complete, birding in the subdivision may become problematical for reasons of both access and habitat change.

Precautions: The main highway here is very heavily traveled and visibility is limited around the curves at the bottom and top of the hill. Even though the shoulder is quite narrow in places, do not stray onto the pavement.

Notable Species:

Nene	Short-eared Owl
Hawaiian Hawk	Saffron Finch
Black Francolin	Yellow-fronted Canary
Erckel's Francolin	Common Amakihi
Kalij Pheasant	Red-cheeked Cordonbleu
Common Pheasant	Lavender Waxbill
Wild Turkey	Black-rumped Waxbill
Mourning Dove	Red Avadavat
Barn Owl	Warbling Silverbill

In terms of number of species, Puu Anahulu is one of Hawaii's greatest birding hot spots. The reason for this distinction is its proximity to Puu Waa Waa Ranch, which was the main release site for game birds introduced by the state and small finches released by the ranch owners. Although many of these species have spread widely, this area remains the most reliable place to find most of them. The habitat is an open, parklike forest of ohia, lama (a native persimmon that somewhat resembles a scrubby ohia), wiliwili (the native coralbean), and the introduced orange-flowered silk oak and purple-flowered jacaranda. In the spring when all the trees are in bloom, the area is really lovely. Grasses and other weeds grow profusely in the open areas between trees and buildings.

Look for Saffron Finches and Yellow-fronted Canaries in the treetops. Also present are surprisingly good numbers of Common Amakihi. The small waxbills and finches are found in grassy places, and their presence depends on what grasses are in what stage of seed development. Be sure to work the entire area from top to bottom, because the birds move around a lot. Warbling Silverbills and Lavender Waxbills are always present on the hillside, but finding the latter may require a little patience. The cordonbleus have been seen most often near the bottom of the hill at the tight road curve. Listen for the thin *see-seee* calls that may be uttered by birds perched on the ground out of sight. Cordonbleus perch in trees more often than the other waxbills, and can sometimes be found in the subdivision. Red Avadavats move around in sometimes huge flocks, and are more often seen in the flat areas above the hillside and in Puu Lani Ranch than on the hillside itself. This is the only reliable locality for Black-rumped Waxbills, but they are not always present and can be maddeningly difficult to pick out of a mixed flock of small finches.

The best place to see the pheasants and francolins is Puu Lani Ranch. Look for them in the open on the mowed shoulders in the early morning and late afternoon. As this area becomes more densely developed, these birds may become shier, but for now this is the best place on the island to see them. Remember to stay in your car; the birds will disappear into the tall grass if you get out. Both species of owl hunt over this area, the Short-eared mainly by day, the Barn Owl mainly at dusk and dawn. Hawaiian Hawks are also occasionally seen soaring overhead. Recently, increasing numbers of Nene have been in the area. They can sometimes be found on the ground in the subdivision, but more often are seen flying over the main highway.

9. Waimea Plains

Location: South Kohala District, between the Saddle Road and the town of Waimea. Detail Map O

Access: Most of the area can be viewed from Mamalahoa Highway (Rt. 190). A private road that is often open leads east off the highway at the West Hawaii Concrete Plant, indicated by a sign at the entrance. This road is about a half mile from the Saddle Road intersection. In the town of Waimea, the Mana Road pond can be reached by taking Rt. 19 toward Hilo from the traffic light in the center of town (if you approach from the Saddle Road end, just go straight through the light). Look for Mana Road to the right. The pond will be visible on the left a short distance from the turnoff, where Mana Road makes a sharp left turn.

Precautions: Be sure not to get locked inside the concrete plant. This is private land, but visitors seem to be well tolerated. As everywhere, avoid stopping on the roadway to view birds; pull off on the shoulder.

Notable Species:

Koloa (Hawaiian Duck)	**Chestnut-bellied Sandgrouse**
Black Francolin	**Short-eared Owl**
Gray Francolin	**Chukar**
Hawaiian Coot	

  The Waimea Plains are a broad expanse of pasturelands that lie just at the break point between the wet windward slope and drier leeward slope of the saddle between Mauna Kea and Kohala Mountain. Most of the land, including the town of Waimea, is included in the Parker Ranch, the largest and one of the oldest in the United

States. This is a good place to look for upland birds of open areas. The star attraction is the Chestnut-bellied Sandgrouse. These unusual birds can be seen flying across the Mamalahoa Highway at dawn and dusk, and occasionally at other times of the day. Two particularly good places to watch for them are near the Waimea-Kohala Airport and in the vicinity of the concrete plant near the Saddle Road. They are most often seen in small to large flocks flying at some distance. The road behind the concrete plant, open between 7 AM and 3 PM, is a good place to look for them on the ground. The area, also favored by shorebirds such as golden plovers and turnstones, looks like the kind of place that could produce a Bristle-thighed Curlew in August or September. (None have been reported, but observers at this site are few.) The Mana Road pond is one of the few places on Hawaii to see Koloa, which have been reintroduced, as well as a good complement of wintering ducks.

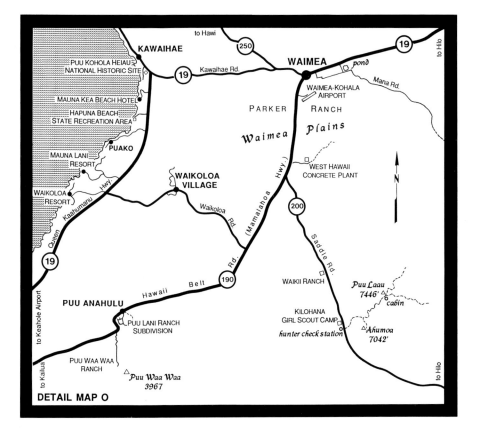

10. Kawaihae and Kohala Coast Resorts

Location: South Kohala District, along Rt. 19 north of Kailua-Kona. Detail Map O.

Access: From Kailua, take the coastal route (Rt. 19, Kaahumanu Highway) north. A chain of luxury resorts are found along the way, the last being Mauna Kea Beach Resort. Most of these allow sightseers in during the day. To reach Kawaihae Harbor, continue north to a T intersection and turn left on Rt. 270 toward Kawaihae; the harbor area is about a mile from this intersection. From Waimea, take Rt. 19 west at the traffic light, then bear left (staying on 19) at the Y intersection and proceed makai seven miles.

Notable Species:

Black Francolin	**Gray Francolin**
Mourning Dove	Yellow-billed Cardinal
Saffron Finch	Warbling Silverbill

Kawaihae Harbor is used by both pleasure boats and commercial shipping. Although usually not very interesting, it can be a good place to look for stray gulls during the winter months. Sometimes waste grain or sand is dumped near the docks in large piles. The piles attract all 4 species of dove including Mourning. Between the 19/270 intersection and the harbor is **Puu Kohola Heiau National Historic Site** which commemorates the founding of the Kingdom of Hawaii by Kamehameha the Great. Birding visitors will appreciate the large numbers of Warbling Silverbills around the park buildings. Below the heiau is a wooded cove where you should see Yellow-billed Cardinals and Gray Francolins. The resorts along the Kohala Coast are man-made oases that attract all of the species listed above. Most of them include artificial bodies of water that are maintained in a near-sterile condition but which sometimes attract vagrant shorebirds. Also worth checking is the village of Waikoloa, mauka off the main highway on a road that connects the coastal route with Mamalahoa Highway.

11. Puu Laau

Location: Above 7,000 feet on leeward slope of Mauna Kea. Detail Map O.

Access: Reached via a side road off the Saddle Road (see introduction for comments about driving on this highway). The easiest access is from the northern (Waimea) end, but the trip from Hilo is not overly long. From Mamalahoa Highway (Rt. 190) about six miles south of Waimea, turn mauka onto the Saddle Road (Rt. 200). Proceed past Waikii Ranch (about six miles up) and begin watching for a compound surrounded by planted evergreen trees on the right (this is Kilohana Girl Scout Camp, but there is no sign). Shortly thereafter you should see a hunter check station on the same side of the road (see photo). If you approach from the Hilo end, just watch for the hunter's kiosk on the left, well beyond the U. S. Army training area at Pohakuloa. Directly opposite the kiosk the road to Puu Laau heads uphill. As of this writing, the road has been graded

and given a semisealed gravel surface that is passable for ordinary vehicles. The road traverses the **Kaohe Game Management Area.** Be sure to stay on the main road. It is not confusing except perhaps at one T-intersection where you should bear sharply left, away from the large cinder cone (Puu Ahumoa) visible to the right. After about four miles, you will see a gate at the boundary of **Mauna Kea Forest Reserve** and a hunter's cabin next to a conspicuous grove of eucalyptus trees. This is the best place to park and explore on foot.

Precautions: Driving on unpaved roads is always "at your own risk." Watch for loose rocks in the roadway, and be sure you know how much clearance your vehicle has. For walking in the mamane-naio forest you should have boots that provide good ankle support. The substrate under the tall grasses is very rocky and irregular, with deep narrow ravines. Because the terrain all looks alike, one can easily become disoriented if fog closes in (which it often does), so do not stray far from the road. Note where the fences are; they can lead you back to your car. Near the cabin, the eucalyptus grove is a good landmark.

Notable Species:

Erckel's Francolin	Melodious Laughing-thrush
Kalij Pheasant	Yellow-fronted Canary
Wild Turkey	**Palila**
California Quail	**Common Amakihi**
Short-eared Owl	Akiapolaau
Elepaio	Iiwi
Red-billed Leiothrix	Apapane

Although a visit requires taking some chances, Puu Laau is well worth a little effort and risk. It is *the* place to see the Palila, the only surviving finch-billed Hawaiian honeycreeper the birder is likely to see, and provides a unique wilderness experience in a habitat difficult to reach elsewhere. The habitat is the mamane-naio forest of the upper slopes of Mauna Kea. It extends in a band around the mountain at about 5,000-8,000 feet but is best developed at Puu Laau. Recent legal actions by the Hawaii Audubon Society and other environmental groups have resulted in the ongoing removal of introduced sheep from the area. These animals, maintained primarily for hunters, were destroying the habitat by eating virtually all seedlings of the dominant mamane and naio trees. Probably as a result of the sheep removal, the annual Palila census reached a ten-year high in 1990. The Palila feeds exclusively on the green seed pods of mamane, a yellow-flowered compound-leaved member of the legume (pea) family. Both it and naio, with glossy green simple leaves, small white flowers, and berry-like white fruits, are shrubby trees that grow fairly widely spaced without forming a closed canopy. It is an open, parklike forest with good visibility and is relatively easy to bird.

As you drive up the road, watch for California Quail. They are often in large coveys and may run down the road ahead of you. Erckel's Francolins and Wild Turkeys are also most easily seen from the car. The best birding begins after about the first mile of dirt road. All of the species listed, including Palila, can be found anywhere along the upper parts of the road. Palila are to some extent nomadic and at some seasons (i. e. October-November) are very quiet and difficult to find, but they are always there. Be patient and listen closely for any whistled calls that seem different from those of House Finches. The Palila's liquid *chee-klee-o*, though not very loud, carries a long way. Calling may be infrequent, so stalk any calls you hear. The birds will allow close approach if you are stealthy, and will probably be closer than you think. They usually travel about in groups of three to five birds. The Palila's call is easy to overlook among the more frequently heard songs and calls of House Finches, skylarks, and Common Amakihi, so learn the more common voices well. The most productive area for Palila over the years has been the hillside just above and behind the hunter's cabin. A dirt track through this area provides easier walking than going cross-country, and can be reached either by following the main road through the eucalyptus grove and turning right just on the other side, or by walking uphill past the outhouse and bearing left.

    Puu Laau is the Common Amakihi capital of the world. They are more abundant here than anywhere else I know, and account for a major percentage of all the birds seen. Probably as a result of their abundance, their calls seem to be more varied here. Sometimes they sound very much like the Palila. This is particularly vexing if you are searching for the very rare Akiapolaau. The bark-picking Aki breeds in low numbers in the mamane-naio forest belt, and is occasionally seen in the vicinity of Puu Laau, but cannot be counted on here. Its call can be surprisingly similar to that of the Palila. Look for a bird like an amakihi with a particularly large head and bill, or any yellow bird that pecks at the bark. Note that amakihi also are sometimes bark-pickers, so try not to have a heart attack every time you see one working the trunks of trees.

    Another Puu Laau specialty is the recently named mamane-naio subspecies of Elepaio. These birds are much paler overall than those from other parts of the Big Island, some having almost all-white heads. They are fairly common, but are skulkers in the dense clumps. Listen for their short, sharp *weet* call and namesake song. Usually a pair or two can be found close to the cabin, and you will likely see them flying across the road ahead of your car (when you will see the white rump and tail tip). Also found skulking near the ground are Red-billed Leiothrix. You will probably hear the loud song of the Melodious Laughing-thrush, but the bird is very difficult to see at Puu Laau.

12. Pohakuloa

Location: Central Saddle Road (Rt. 200) in flats at base of Mauna Kea.

Access: Open to the public. The Saddle Road passes through the area. A picnic ground and rustic cabins are at Mauna Kea State Park just east (Hilo side) of Pohakuloa Military Camp (a training facility closed to the public). A pay phone and public restrooms are available at the state park.

Precautions: Be careful of military traffic entering from side roads. Remember that there are no service stations or stores anywhere on the Saddle Road, so bring what you think you will need and be sure you have plenty of gas.

Notable Species:

Black Francolin	**Red-billed Leiothrix**
Erckel's Francolin	Northern Mockingbird
Chukar	Common Amakihi
California Quail	**Warbling Silverbill**

Although not a major birding locality in its own right, Pohakuloa has a few interesting things to offer the birder passing through to or from other Saddle Road localities. The name applies to a large flat area at the base of Mauna Kea that represents the highest part of the Saddle Road. When most people use the name, however, they are referring to the detached Pohakuloa Section of **Mauna Kea State Park.** Most of the park is at higher elevation on the mountain. Along the highway, look for various game birds. All of those listed can be seen, but Erckel's Francolins are probably the most common. California Quail are usually seen within a mile on either side of the picnic grounds, and sometimes come onto the lawns there. Because this area is usually very dry, any source of water will attract birds. Two water drips in the backyard of the caretaker's residence attract Warbling Silverbills,

House Finches, Common Amakihi, and Red-billed Leiothrix. To reach them, bear left as you enter the park and follow the paved road around to the back and look on the left behind a low fence. The water drips are easily visible from the public side of the fence, so you need not disturb the privacy of park personnel. One faucet is near the middle of the yard, the other under a dense evergreen tree close to the fence. Be patient and do not stand too close to the spigots. Leiothrix dart in quickly and then disappear into the surrounding scrub, but you may get a better look here than anywhere. Another water drip (sometimes) is from an overhead standpipe near the end of the entrance road pavement.

13. Saddle Road Kipukas

Location: Along the Hilo end of the Saddle Road (Rt. 200) from about 3500 feet elevation to Puu Huluhulu. Detail Map P.

Access: The various kipukas can be reached by the Saddle Rd., Puu Oo Trail, and Powerline Rd. To reach most of those along the main highway, you will have to hike across some rather hostile terrain. Many of them have "unofficial" footpaths leading in. Puu Oo Trail provides easier access to several large kipukas off the highway. The trailhead is on the south (Mauna Loa) side of the highway just on the Hilo side of the boundary of Upper Waiakea Forest Reserve, which is marked. There is a trail sign at a small parking area, but it is easy to miss from the highway, so drive slowly while looking for it. The trail is obvious in the kipukas, but on lava flows is marked by cairns (conical piles of rocks) and sometimes flagging tape. Just short of four miles from the highway, the trail merges with Powerline Road, a gravel jeep road. Beyond this point both the trail and Powerline Road are blocked by the 1984 lava flow. You can return to the Saddle Road more quickly by taking the jeep road, but it is a much less interesting walk. Powerline Road enters the Saddle Road a little less than a mile below the Puu Oo trailhead. It, too, has a sign. Allow at least four hours for the round trip.

A particularly accessible kipuka is just below the Powerline Road intersection. Watch for the point where the powerlines cross over the Saddle Road just above a sharp curve. A large grove of trees with several prominent emergent koas will be on the north side of the highway (see illustration). A very rough jeep track takes off from the road at a sharp angle and immediately descends for about a hundred yards. Walk down this track and watch for a footpath to the left at the bottom of the hill through a small group of koa saplings. This will take you down to the floor of the kipuka. There is room to park off the highway at the upper end of the jeep track.

Precautions: Walking over lava flows, particularly aa, is always treacherous. Watch your step; lava cuts are ragged and slow to heal. Good hiking boots with ankle support are essential. Be sure you can retrace your steps on the Puu Oo Trail without reference to distant landmarks. These may be obscured by frequent afternoon fog. The power poles along Powerline Rd. have been removed, so no longer provide a reference point. No water is available in this area; bring plenty. Temperatures can vary widely with changing weather conditions, so bring a wrap and a raincoat.

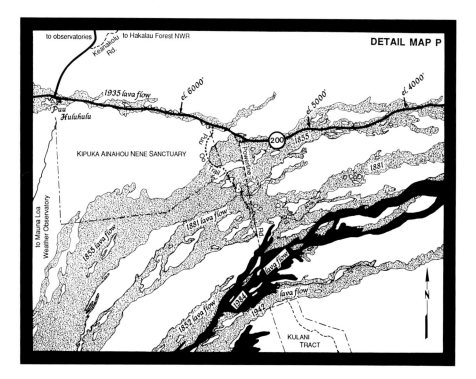

Notable Species:

Nene	Akiapolaau
Hawaiian Hawk	Hawaii Creeper
Elepaio	Akepa
Omao	Iiwi
Red-billed Leiothrix	Apapane
Common Amakihi	

Kipukas are islands of older forest surrounded by younger lava flows. They are fascinating islands of nearly pristine vegetation that have been protected by the surrounding lava from invasion by alien plants and herbivores (although some pigs are present). From the Saddle Road, they look like low groves of tree growing on the lava. It is only when one approaches the edge that their true nature is revealed. The "low" trees are actually the upper canopy of centuries-old forest giants. To enter these wonderlands, one must descend from the surrounding lava, a sometimes difficult task. It is well worth the effort, however, as you will find a nearly all-native plant community with mostly native birds (the only alien that is at all common here is the Japanese White-eye). Iiwi are abundant, and Omao can be heard all around. The Elepaio here belong to the darkest subspecies, quite different from those at Puu Laau (Hawaii 11). Unfortunately, the rarer birds cannot be found in the kipukas close to the road with any regularity. Akiapolaau, Akepa, and Hawaii Creeper can be seen along Puu Oo Trail and Powerline Road, but are easier to find elsewhere. Nene and Hawaiian Hawk are sometimes seen as fly-overs. Even without the prospect of seeing the rarer species, the kipukas are well worth a visit by anyone who appreciates beautiful unspoiled forests. The kipukas are the closest thing we have to a time capsule of prehistoric Hawaii.

14. Hakalau Forest National Wildlife Refuge

Location: Eastern slope of Mauna Kea, above the Hamakua Coast.

Access: Closed to the public. This newly established refuge is understaffed and open only under permit. Organized tours may be able to arrange a visit, but individuals unfamiliar with the area will not be allowed to enter unescorted. This policy may change in the future. For up-to-date information, write to the Refuge Manager, Hakalau Forest NWR, 154 Waianuenue Ave., Rm. 219, Hilo, HI 96720 or phone (808) 969-9909. To reach the refuge from either end of the Saddle Road (Rt. 200), watch for a large forested cinder cone (Puu Huluhulu) on the Mauna Loa side of the highway. Then look for a wide paved road entering from the Mauna Kea side directly opposite a hunter check station at the base of Puu Huluhulu. This is the access road to the observatories at the summit of Mauna Kea. Follow this road uphill past a ranch complex on the right and take the first open gravel road to the right. This is Keanakolu Road (no sign), a county road open to the public but recommended for four-wheel-drive vehicles only. Depending on how the weather has been and how recently the road was graded, you may be able to use an ordinary vehicle. About 45 minutes from the Saddle Road, look for a ranch road heading downhill to a gate emblazoned with the name Pua Akala. This gate is locked, but the walk (about .75 mile) to the refuge from Keanakolu Road is not difficult.

Precautions: Entering the refuge without permission constitutes trespassing. If you are able to arrange a visit, be very careful not to disturb the camps, nets, and other research equipment in the area. If researchers are present, ask them what areas you should avoid. Keep in mind that future public access to this wonderful birding area will depend in large part on whether such access is compatible with ongoing research on native birds. Do not attempt to drive on Keanakolu Road in an ordinary vehicle unless you have up-to-date information that it is safe to do so. Be prepared for bad weather; it can come in surprisingly fast and road conditions can change suddenly. Washouts are frequent.

Notable Species:

Koloa (Hawaiian Duck)	**Omao**	
Hawaiian Hawk	Red-billed Leiothrix	
Erckel's Francolin	Common Amakihi	
Chukar	**Akiapolaau**	
Kalij Pheasant	**Hawaii Creeper**	
Wild Turkey	**Akepa**	
California Quail	**Iiwi**	
Gambel's Quail	Apapane	
Elepaio		

Hakalau Forest is the first national wildlife refuge to be established solely for the management of forest birds. The initial tract was acquired by The Nature Conservancy and sold to the U. S. Fish and Wildlife Service. This nucleus has been expanded to include some surrounding areas which now comprise almost 16,500 acres. The refuge preserves some of the finest montane koa/ohia forest remaining on the Big Island. Unfortunately, the refuge, like many others, suffers from limited funding and does not yet have sufficient personnel and infrastructure to support public access. The staff has its hands full just supervising removal of feral cattle (the area was originally a cattle ranch) and pigs, re-establishing native forest, controlling weeds, and helping ornithologists studying there. The restrictions on visitation are reasonable and should be respected. Perhaps if enough birders express interest, government sources will provide sufficient support to allow for supervised public access to this important refuge.

Hakalau Forest harbors at least four endangered forest birds (Hawaiian Hawk, Akiapolaau, Hawaii Creeper, and Akepa). Akepa are abundant, and Hawaii Creepers are relatively easy to find. Akiapolaau are less common, but can be found with a little persistence. The most common honeycreeper here is the Iiwi, outnumbering even Common Amakihi and Apapane. Also numerous are Omao and Elepaio. The hawk is usually seen soaring overhead, and is not confined to the refuge itself; look for it along Keanakolu Road. Kalij Pheasants and Wild Turkeys are found mostly in the open grassy areas at the upper edge of the forest.

On the drive in to the refuge, look for game birds including both Gambel's and California quail. This is one of the few places on Hawaii that Gambel's Quail has been seen regularly. Check the ranch ponds for ducks, most of which will be reintroduced Koloa. Between October and April, a few migratory ducks show up as well. Chukar and turkeys are also easy to see in the open ranch lands along the road. The best time of day to visit this area is early morning, when the weather is usually clear. Clouds roll in by midday, and rain is frequent in the afternoon. Under some conditions, rain may persist all day for long periods.

HURRICANE INIKI UPDATE

In September 1992, while this book was in press, Hurricane Iniki struck Kauai with devastating force. Winds has high as 225 mph were reported at Kokee! I was able to spend 3 days on Kauai in October to assess what the storm will mean for birders. Visitors to Kauai for the next few years should read this update carefully and interpret the accounts accordingly. Destruction was island-wide; few buildings escaped damage and many homes and businesses were completely destroyed. As of this writing (December 1992), most hotels are still closed and some will remain so for as much as 3 years. At Kilauea Point (Site 2), both the book shop next to the lighthouse and the brand new visitor center were virtually destroyed, and the refuge is temporarily closed. How soon public visitation may resume is impossible to say. Buildings at Kokee (Site 10) fared better, and presumably will reopen after electricity is restored.

Kauai's legendary greenery was so severely altered that many years will pass before the Garden Isle even approaches its pre-Iniki appearance. Huleia Stream Valley (Site 5), which was so noted for its jungle-like appearance that it was used for some scenes in the movie *Raiders of the Lost Ark*, was completely denuded as was Keahua Arboretum (Site 1). Nearly every large tree at both sites was either downed or stripped by the storm. Throughout the island, forests of alien trees such as eucalyptus, albizzia, or silk oak were levelled. Native montane koa and ohia forests did better but were nevertheless severely impacted. Most of the forest canopy on exposed ridges was removed. Many old trees were downed, but few were killed outright and vegetation in deep ravines came through the storm nearly undamaged. The more remote hiking trails will be blocked by blown-over trees for a long time. Because of the severe fire hazard caused by the presence of so much dead wood, the Camp 10 (Mohihi) Rd. has been closed to vehicular traffic just beyond the Puu Ka Ohelo Trailhead. Until this road reopens, I recommend that birders use the Pihea Ridge Trail (Site 10) to access the Kawaikoi Stream area. The new boardwalks on this and the Alakai Swamp Trail were ripped up in places by the roots of overturned trees, but are still in surprisingly good condition.

Iniki may have delivered a death blow to some of Kauai's extremely rare native birds. I am particularly worried that the few remaining Ou, which are fruit-eaters, may not have been able to find sufficient food after the storm to survive. None of the very rare birds (Ou, Nukupuu, Kamao, Puaiohi) have been seen since Iniki; all future sightings of them are extremely important and should be reported. The good news is that the more common bird species survived the storm, though in reduced numbers, and can still be found in the same areas as before. We were able to find all but the rarest species 6 weeks after Iniki. Rental cars are still available, all paved roads have been cleared, and restaurants and lodgings are slowly reopening so birders have no reason to skip Kauai. The local tourist industry certainly needs your business. Keep in mind, however, that some sites will look drastically different from their pre-Iniki conditions.

Kauai

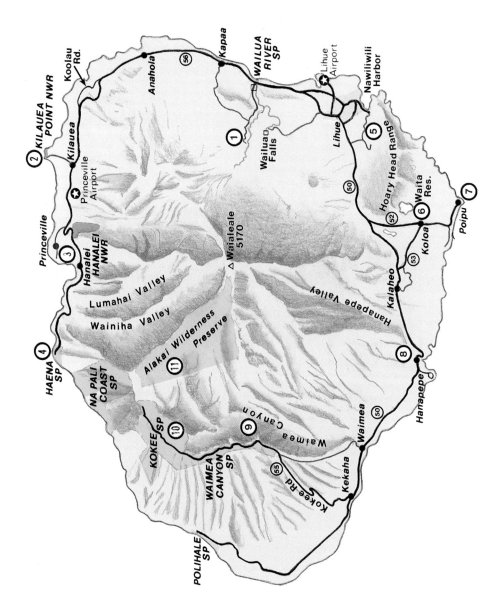

KAUAI

Kauai is geologically the oldest of the main Hawaiian Islands. Millions of years of erosion have nearly obliterated the configuration of its original volcano. The deep red soil of the Garden Isle, as it is known, contrasts stunningly with its lush green vegetation. The islandwide lushness is attributable to Kauai's abundant rainfall and the fact that only a tiny "rain shadow" exists on the island itself (but covers the entire island of Niihau). The highest peak, Waialeale, which forms the high point on the distant pali behind Lihue, is often considered the world's wettest spot with around 34 feet (yes, that's *feet*, not inches) of annual rainfall. From the peak of Waialeale a high plateau sweeps northwestward. Although not as rainy as the peak itself, this area is so wet that it is often called the Alakai Swamp (although not a true swamp). At the western end of the Alakai Wilderness Preserve (Site 10) lies the Kokee (correctly pronounced with three syllables: *ko-KEH-eh*; most people just make it rhyme with OK; whatever you do, don't make it rhyme with *okie*) region (Site 9). Streams draining the Alakai and Kokee areas have carved deep valleys that coalesce into Waimea Canyon (Site 8), one of the scenic wonders of the Pacific. Kokee and the Alakai Plateau provide some of the best birding in Hawaii, although not as good as it used to be. Until the 1970s, Kauai had the distinction of not having lost any of its historically known native birds. The first to go was the Akialoa, last seen in 1969 by Phil Bruner. All the others could still be found in the depths of the Alakai into the mid-1970s. From then on, however, the birds were on a downhill slide. The Kauai Oo passed into extinction around 1988 (the exact date when the last one died will never be known), and Kauai's two endemic solitaires, the Kamao and Puaiohi, are each probably now down to under twenty individuals. The Ou population, in the hundreds in 1975, has crashed to a few pairs and the Nukupuu, always rare, remains so. Nevertheless, Kauai remains the place where one can find more native forest birds in one place than anywhere else in Hawaii. Several Kauai endemics (Anianiau, Kauai Amakihi, Akekee) are still common in places and another (Akikiki) can be found with some diligent searching. Because it is the only main island to lack mongooses, Kauai is also the last stronghold for several ground-nesting native water birds and the Red Junglefowl, descended from chickens brought by the first Hawaiians. The north shore of the island is noted for its beautiful beaches, estuaries, and palis. Kilauea Point (Site 2), at about 2 o'clock on the Kauai clock-face, is one of the most accessible places in Hawaii for viewing nesting seabirds.

Kauai is nearly circular, with one main highway that does not completely encircle the island (you will see why when you approach the gap from either end). Tourism has belatedly caught up with once laid-back Kauai and traffic jams are now a daily annoyance. Accommodations for visitors are concentrated in three main areas: Lihue-Kapaa on the east coast; Princeville-Hanalei on the north shore; and Poipu on the south coast. Because the island is relatively small, all of these are convenient for birding. The main airport is in Lihue, but Princeville has a smaller commuter airport.

Common and Widespread Birds

White-tailed Tropicbird
Cattle Egret
Black-crowned Night-Heron
Red Junglefowl
Hawaiian Coot
Pacific Golden-Plover*
Rock Dove
Spotted Dove
Zebra Dove

White-rumped Shama
Northern Mockingbird
Common Myna
Japanese White-eye
Northern Cardinal
House Finch
House Sparrow
Nutmeg Mannikin
Chestnut Mannikin

*seasonal

1. Wailua River Valley

Location: East coast of Kauai, about six miles north of Lihue. Detail Map Q.

Access: All areas can be reached by public highway. From Lihue, head north on Rt. 56. After crossing the bridge over the mouth of the Wailua River (the first large river you come to), turn left at the traffic light (the Coco Palms Resort is in the northwest corner of this intersection). You will then be on Kuamoo Road (Rt. 580). Just past the Coco Palms on the right are the Wailua Flats, an area of marshes and cultivated fields. The road continues uphill to a parking area for viewing Opaekaa Falls. Continue mauka on the road through a residential area known as Wailua Homesteads. Once past the houses, look for Wailua Reservoir, a large body of water on the right. Although the reservoir is close to the road, it is only visible at a few points. You can park at several places and walk to the edge of the water. Following Rt. 580 further, you will enter Keahua Arboretum. The road is paved (but very badly maintained) through the arboretum but eventually turns to dirt, where you should turn around.

Notable Species: Koloa (Hawaiian Duck)
Common Moorhen
Japanese Bush-Warbler
Greater Necklaced Laughing-thrush
Melodious Laughing-thrush
Western Meadowlark

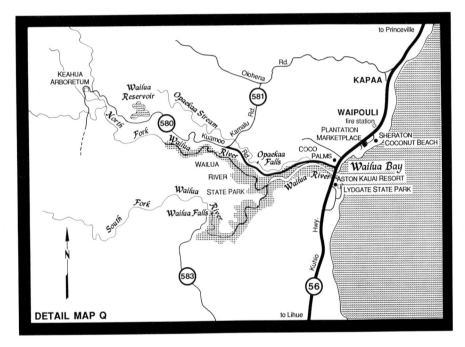

The Wailua River Valley, because of its spectacular beauty, is a major tourist stop. The tour buses go no further than Opaekaa Falls, however, so birders can still have the best parts of the valley nearly to themselves. The **Wailua Flats** attract freshwater birds, including Koloa, Common Moorhens, Black-necked Stilts, and Hawaiian Coots. The coots can be seen anywhere on the rivers and reservoirs in the area. The overlook for **Opaekaa Falls** (shown above) is a wonderful place to view White-tailed Tropicbirds, which nest in the cliffs across the valley, against a scenic backdrop. **Wailua Reservoir** is a good place to look for wintering waterfowl, especially diving ducks such as scaup and Ring-necks. The upper reaches of the valley, and especially **Keahua Arboretum**, provide excellent habitat for shamas and both laughing-thrushes. The Greater Necklaced Laughing-thrush, being nomadic, is not always present but has been seen here more than once. This is also the easiest place on Kauai to find Japanese Bush-Warblers.

2. Kilauea Point National Wildlife Refuge

Location: Northernmost point on Kauai. Detail Map R.

Access: Open to the public 10 AM-4 PM daily except Saturday. Admission $2 for adults (the best $2 you will spend in Hawaii!). Golden Eagle and Golden Age passes accepted. From the airport in Lihue, drive north on Kuhio Highway (Rt. 56) and take either turnoff for the village of Kilauea (the second one is easiest). Take the street running makai from the tiny Episcopal church made of lava rock and follow it all the way out to the refuge. Entrance fees are collected at a booth above the parking lot on the way to the lighthouse.

Notable Species:

Laysan Albatross	Great Frigatebird
Wedge-tailed Shearwater	Barn Owl
Red-tailed Tropicbird	Short-eared Owl
Brown Booby	Melodious Laughing-thrush
Red-footed Booby	Western Meadowlark

Kilauea Point is *the* place for seabirds in Hawaii. The grounds surrounding the lighthouse were administered by the Coast Guard for years and formed a *de facto* refuge. When the lighthouse was automated, the land was transferred to the Fish and Wildlife Service who have made it into a showcase refuge, now the nation's most visited. Once overgrown with weed plants, the point has been completely replanted in native vegetation, including some species from the uninhabited Northwestern Hawaiian Islands. Recent additions of land to the east more than doubled the size of the refuge. These new additions are not open to the public full time, but docent-led hikes into the area are offered several times a week. Inquire at the visitor center or write to the Refuge Manager (P. O. Box 87, Kilauea, Kauai, HI 96754) for a schedule. Although you can see all the bird species of the point in the lighthouse area, the hikes are well worth the effort because the views from Crater Hill east of the point are among Kauai's most spectacular. Cats and dogs had long been a problem at Kilauea Point because of the proximity of human residential areas, but a new fence has helped tremendously in keeping these predators out. Laysan Albatrosses had attempted for years to nest at Kilauea but had always lost their chicks to predation. Now more than forty pairs breed here, the only viable albatross colony on any of the main Hawaiian Islands. Wedge-tailed Shearwaters nest in burrows within inches of paved walkways, and some even nest on the surface under the dense *Scaevola* bushes. Between late March and October, they can usually be seen any time of day around the lighthouse area, even though most of their goings and comings are at dawn and dusk. Their low moaning cries are useful in locating birds under the shrubbery. Red-tailed Tropicbirds are common and conspicuous from March through September; a few hang around all year but are highly unreliable in the off-season. In the spring, they put on quite a show with their acrobatic courtship flights. The best place to view them is the outermost point, where birds fly in from the open water and catch the updraft from the cliff. They sometimes pop up within a few feet of the observer. Bring your camera. White-tailed Tropicbirds are also present but the Red-tails are more common during the breeding season. Another first-class performance is put on by the frigatebirds as they harass the Red-footed Boobies coming in to feed chicks. The Red-foots nest in trees on the mainland, but Brown Boobies are ground nesters that have not yet taken advantage of Kilauea Point's protected status.

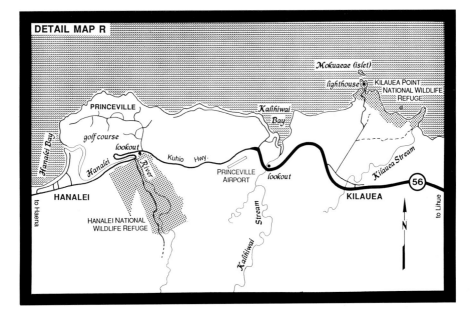

They nest only on Moku Aeae, the islet that can be seen from the lighthouse. A spotting scope is useful for viewing the islet (you can borrow one from the nearby visitor center). Even though the refuge is closed long before dusk, much of the area can still be viewed from the lookout at the entrance gate. Just before and after sunset you can see shearwaters returning to their burrows and sometimes owls. Both Barn Owls and Short-eared Owls can be seen on the refuge and hunting over nearby pastures. Owls (probably Barn) are suspected in some of the recent deaths of albatross chicks. Recently, Kilauea Point has gained a new attraction with the release of captive-reared Nene. Nene are known to have lived on Kauai in prehistoric times, so these may be regarded as a reintroduction. Perhaps the protected area within the refuge will enable the Nene to re-establish a wild population on this mongoose-free island. The released birds are quite tame and often accompany hikers on the trek to Crater Hill.

3. Princeville and Hanalei

Location: At the midpoint of Kauai's north shore, on the eastern side of Hanalei Bay. Detail Map R.

Access: Reached via Rt. 56 north from Lihue. After passing Kilauea, Kalihiwai Valley, and Princeville Airport, begin watching for the main entrance to Princeville on the right. A shopping center is just beyond the intersection. Numerous roads wind through the golf courses and residential developments of Princeville. Back on the main highway, about a hundred yards beyond the shopping center is an overlook on the left where the taro fields of Hanalei National Wildlife Refuge (pictured above) may be viewed. Ahead, the road doubles back sharply as it descends to the Hanalei River. Just across the bridge at the bottom is a narrow paved road to the left which will take you into the wildlife refuge. This road is open to the public, but entry into the agricultural areas on either side is restricted. Wilcox Pond may be reached by taking the first street makai in Hanalei Village, then turning right at the T intersection. At the end of this street is a beach park on the left and a parking area, from which the pond can be viewed, on the right.

Precautions: The road into Hanalei NWR is very narrow with few places for vehicles to pass. Try not to block the road when you stop to view birds.

Notable Species: Koloa (Hawaiian Duck)
Common Moorhen
Black-necked Stilt
Western Meadowlark

Because Princeville is almost the first landfall for birds migrating to Hawaii from the north, it is a good place to look for unusual shorebirds. The golf courses are inhabited by Pacific Golden-Plovers, Western Meadowlarks, Cattle Egrets, and numerous doves. Among them is an occasional diamond-in-the-rough. Kauai's only record of Buff-breasted Sandpiper was on the Princeville Golf Course. Be sure to stop at the Hanalei NWR overlook. It is a good place to scope out the whole refuge to locate concentrations of waterfowl or shorebirds. The fields directly below on the eastern side of the river (to your left from the overlook) are not readily visible from the lower road, so you will have to settle for this distant view. A spotting scope is essential. The crop being grown is taro, the root of which is made into the traditional Hawaiian dish called poi. Most of the poi consumed today is made from Hanalei taro. Hanalei NWR is an example of unusually creative thinking on the part of the U. S. Fish and Wildlife Service. These taro fields were slated for "development" (=destruction) and the local farmers, who had leased the land for generations, were about to be displaced along with several endangered species of Hawaiian water birds that depend on such artificial habitats for survival today. In a beautiful arrangement, the government acquired the land for a wildlife refuge with the understanding that the farmers could remain (after all, the farmers created the habitat). Taro is grown on a rotational basis and the fields are flooded mainly to discourage the growth of weeds. At any given time, there will be fields in all stages of rotation that provide both mudflats and freshwater ponds. Native Koloa and many wintering ducks (mostly Northern Shovelers and Northern Pintails) as well as coots, moorhens, night-herons, and stilts use the ponds. During April-May and September-October, migratory shorebirds are sometimes present in the muddy fields. An added surprise between the refuge and the town of Hanalei is a farm on the right that raises American bison. Wilcox Pond is privately owned but can be easily viewed from outside the fence. Hawaiian Coots, Common Moorhens, and Hawaiian Ducks on the pond are joined by wintering ducks October-March. American Coots have been found here in the past.

4. Haena State Park

Location: North shore of Kauai at terminus of Rt. 56.

Access: Open to the public. From Lihue, take Rt. 56 all the way to the end. It is a slow trip, so allow a couple of hours each way.

Precautions: The road beyond Hanalei Bay is narrow and winding with numerous one-lane bridges. Many drivers are distracted by the spectacular scenery and forget that they are on a highway. Drive defensively. Pull off the highway if you want to pause, especially around blind curves. Beaches in this area are very popular, especially on weekends. Parking is limited at Haena State Park, so weekdays are the best times for birding visits.

Notable Species:

Laysan Albatross	Brown Noddy
Wedge-tailed Shearwater	Black Noddy
Red-footed Booby	White-rumped Shama
Brown Booby	Melodious Laughing-thrush

Haena State Park is worth a visit even if you see no birds. At the end of the road is a small bay at Kee Beach with calm reef-protected water that is popular for snorkeling. In the trees near the restrooms, look for Melodious Laughing-thrushes foraging thrasher-like in the leaf litter. On the mauka side of the road is the trailhead of the eleven-mile **Kalalau Trail** to Kalalau Valley. Along this trail is the only known locality for Red-billed Leiothrix on Kauai. For a spectacular view of the **Na Pali Coast**, walk back along the beach (to the right from the end of the road) about two hundred yards. Here you can see boobies, noddies, and albatrosses flying fairly close to shore. Brown Boobies may even come in to the shallow water inside the reef. This is also one of the few places on

Kauai to regularly find Black Noddies, which nest in the remote Na Pali cliffs. In the spring, spectacular numbers of shearwaters congregate offshore, but most will be tantalizingly distant—close enough to be seen with a high-power scope but too far out for species identification. A number of tour companies offer Zodiac boat trips offshore along the Na Pali coast, but they do not venture far enough out to be of much help with the distant seabirds. However, they can provide spectacular views of Black Noddies.

5. Huleia Stream Valley

Location: Southeastern Kauai between Lihue and Haupu (Hoary Head) Range. Detail Map S.

Access: Most areas are on public roads. Huleia NWR is closed but can be viewed from the periphery at several places. From Lihue, the area can be approached from two directions that make a loop. From the airport, take the first left onto Kapule Highway (Rt. 51) and follow it to a T intersection. Turn left here onto Wapaa Road (also Rt. 51) toward Nawiliwili Harbor. Remain on this road as it winds through the harbor complex (follow signs for Menehune Fishpond) and eventually becomes Hulemalu Road at its intersection with Niumalu. As the road ascends the hill and curves sharply to the right, look for an overlook on the left from which you can view Alakoko Pond (shown above). Continue on Hulemalu in the same direction through sugar cane fields. Watch for a bridge over a small stream and take the next road to the left, Haiku Road. This road descends into the valley and makes very sharp turn to the right. From that point until it ends, the road skirts Huleia NWR on the left. At the end of the pavement is a private driveway to the left. You can turn around here and park on the right as you head outward, making sure you do not block the road or driveway. Walk the few hundred yards beyond the end of the pavement to a stone bridge on Huleia Stream. To make a loop, return to Hulemalu, turn left, and follow it to its T intersection with Kipu Road. A right turn here will take you a short distance to the main highway (Rt. 50). Turn right to return to Lihue or left for points west. To execute the loop in reverse, take Rt. 50 out of Lihue and turn left onto Kipu Road after you pass Kauai Community College on the

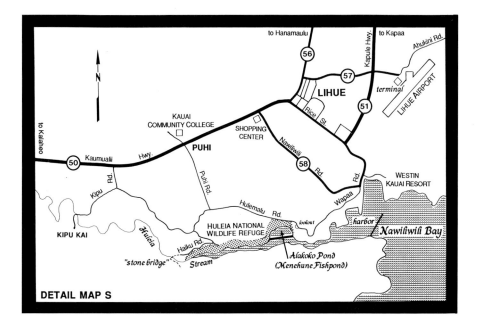

DETAIL MAP S

right. The first road to the left will be Hulemalu. Kipu Road continues to the right, crosses Huleia Stream and ends at several private roads.

Precautions: The gardens on either side of Haiku Rd. are private. Some of them are in the traditional Polynesian style and look like natural forest, but crops are being raised nevertheless. Please respect the property of these traditional farmers. Birding should be done only along the roadway itself, but try not to block the road. Mosquito repellent may be needed on the walk to the stone bridge on Huleia Stream.

Notable Species: Koloa (Hawaiian Duck)   Melodious Laughing-thrush
                        White-rumped Shama   Greater Necklaced Laughing-
                                                        thrush

Huleia National Wildlife Refuge is an as yet undeveloped refuge for Hawaiian water birds. It includes the lower reaches of Huleia Stream and **Alakoko Pond**, popularly known as Menehune Fishpond. The pond almost always has a few Koloa and during the winter months you may find migratory ducks. It is also a good place to look for Ospreys, although they are by no means always present. The upper end of the refuge along **Haiku Road** is a lovely junglelike area that is one of the best places to see shamas and both species of laughing-thrush. The Melodious can sometimes be seen sitting in the road ahead of your vehicle. Greater Necklaced Laughing-thrushes are more elusive and can be seen either skulking in the underbrush or foraging quietly along the upper branches of tall trees. The tops of several huge flat-topped monkeypod trees downslope from the road can be viewed at eye level and should always be investigated. The big laughing-thrushes are not always present, but this is the most reliable locality for them. If you strike out on Haiku Road, try taking Kipu Road to its end. Check the large trees at the bridge over Huleia Stream. The open fields just beyond the bridge nearly always have Western Meadowlarks.

6. Waita Reservoir

Location: South of Rt. 50 near Koloa. Detail Map T.

Access: From Lihue, take Rt. 50 west and turn south at the "Tunnel of Trees" onto Maluhia Road (Rt. 53) toward Koloa. Just as the town comes into view, look for Wailaau Road entering from the left just north of a large athletic field. If you reach the fire station, you have gone too far. Turn left onto Wailaau and follow it until it crosses a small bridge and curves sharply to the right. Immediately after the curve, look for a small unmarked road to the left. The road is blocked by large boulders a short distance in, but provides a convenient place to park. Walk to the left past the boulders and follow the cane haul road through a locked yellow gate. The reservoir will come into view on the right after about a half-mile walk. A little further in you will see a couple of side ponds on the left. From Poipu or Koloa, take Rt. 53 toward Lihue and look for Wailaau Road just past the fire station and athletic field on the right. It will be the next right after Emi Road. The gravel roads are private, but are not posted at present.

Precautions: Be careful not to block the gravel roads or gates. The less nuisance birders create here, the better for future access. Formerly one could drive to the reservoir, so the access situation is unclear as of this writing. Presumably birders may walk in, as local fishermen do, past the recently-erected gate.

Notable Species: Koloa (Hawaiian Duck)
Hawaiian Coot
Black-necked Stilt

Waita (pronounce both syllables with equal stress) **Reservoir** is the largest body of fresh water on Kauai. [The name is from an older form of the Hawaiian language wherein *t* represented the sound that became the *k* in more recent Hawaiian. Kauai was

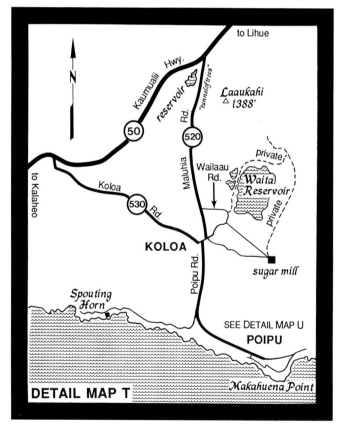

the last island to make the *t* to *k* shift.] It is also one of the deepest, and for that reason is a good place to look for diving ducks in winter. Scaup and Ring-necks are regular, and such rarities as Tufted Duck and Canvasback should be looked for. Water levels fluctuate with weather and the needs of the sugar growers, so Waita can be rather unpredictable. Some years it boasts spectacular concentrations of wintering waterfowl, other years it is barren. Also depending on the amount of water present, the side ponds to the left of the cane road can be very good for migrant shorebirds in spring and fall (April and October seem to be the peaks). Sharp-tailed, Pectoral, and Least sandpipers are good possibilities. When conditions are right, the three native species listed above can be abundant.

7. Makahuena Point

Location: South coast of Kauai in Poipu. Detail Maps T and U.

Access: From Rt. 50 west of Lihue take either Maluhia Road (Rt. 52) south through the "tunnel of trees" or Koloa Road (Rt. 53) to Koloa, then head south on Poipu Road. At a prominent Y intersection, take the left fork, staying on Poipu Road. After you pass the entrance to Stouffer Waiohai Beach Resort on the right, take the next right onto Hoowili Road. This forms a T intersection shortly with Hoone Road. Turn left and follow Hoone Road until the main road makes a sharp uphill left turn and becomes Pee (*Peh-eh*) Road. Look for the Poipu-at-Makahuena condominiums, then a cluster of old cinder-block white buildings, both on the right. Turn in at the white buildings and make an immediate right into a small parking area. You can park here or follow the road through the lot and around to the left for a short distance to the end of the pavement. Follow the dirt road on foot a short distance to the headland atop Makahuena Point. Do not disturb the residents of the cinder-block buildings, which are private.

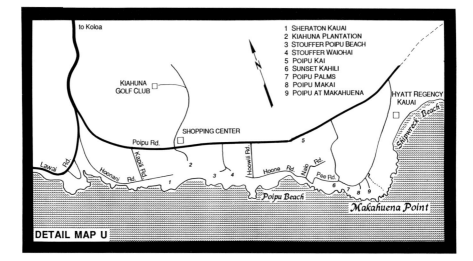

Notable Species: Laysan Albatross   Townsend's (Newell's)
                     Hawaiian (Dark-rumped)   Shearwater
                       Petrel   Brown Booby
                     Bulwer's Petrel   Red-footed Booby
                     Wedge-tailed Shearwater   Brown Noddy

    Makahuena Point extends further out into the Kauai Channel than any other land and is thus an excellent place to watch for passing seabirds. A good spotting scope is probably a necessity here. This locality has not been well birded, so what can be found at various seasons is not really known. Anything could turn up. In April and early May, at least, hundreds of Wedge-tailed Shearwaters, a few Townsend's Shearwaters, and a sprinkling of Hawaiian (Dark-rumped) and Bulwer's Petrels can be seen far offshore, especially late in the day. A nearby area that is also worth checking (if not for birds, for great scenery) is **Kamala Point.** To reach it, continue on Poipu Road past the turnoff to Makahuena Point. Proceed past the posh new Hyatt Regency Kauai Resort set apart from the main cluster of condos and turn right at the first cross road. [As of this writing, some construction is still proceeding in this area, so these directions may not remain accurate. Inquire locally.] This will end at a maze of unpaved tracks that provide access to various parts of the point and nearby beaches. Hawaiian monk seals have been reported here recently.

8. Hanapepe Area

Location: Southwest coast of Kauai between Kalaheo and Waimea. Detail Map V.

Access: From the east, take Kaumualii Highway (Rt. 50) through Kalaheo. Look for a paved overlook on the right where you can view Hanapepe Valley. Continue ahead to Eleele. Just before a sharp curve to the right (a shopping center will be straight ahead but on the left side of the road) you can turn left to Port Allen and proceed straight ahead to the harbor area. To reach the agricultural fields in lower Hanapepe Valley, take the first right around the sharp curve to the right past the turn-off to Port Allen. This is Hanapepe Road, the main commercial street of the town of Hanapepe. The first paved road to the right (mauka) off this street is Ko Road, a passable dirt track through the agricultural area. The road eventually reaches a locked gate. On the return trip, look for a turn to the right that crosses the Hanapepe River at a ford. You can make a loop by turning left onto paved Awaawa Road, which takes you back to Hanapepe Rd. and the main highway. At the far end of town, look for a left turn marked by a King Kamehameha point of interest sign labelled "Ancient Salt Pans." Turn left here onto Lele Road. At the Kauai Veterans Cemetery on the right, the road forks. You can take either side because these roads connect to form a loop. The right fork takes you more directly to the salt pans, the left passes a small airstrip first.

Notable Species: Great Frigatebird   Rose-ringed Parakeet
Common Pheasant   Short-eared Owl
Black-necked Stilt   Western Meadowlark

131

The Hanapepe Valley overlook is one of the best places to look for Rose-ringed Parakeets. They often fly by in small groups in the early morning but can be seen any time of day. This is also a beautiful spot to study White-tailed Tropicbirds at eye level. Watch for Short-eared Owls in the valley as well as over the agricultural fields makai of the overlook. The harbor at Port Allen is not usually very interesting, but during winter months should always be checked for the occasional stray gull. Great Frigatebirds often soar over the bay. The back roads through lower Hanapepe Valley provide access to fields where Rose-ringed Parakeets have been reported to be pests (particularly in fields of green corn). A small pond on the left near the start of Ko Road may harbor Common Moorhens, and Black-crowned Night-herons are frequent along the river.

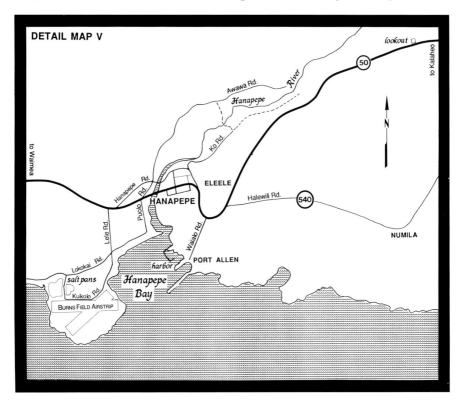

The salt pans are shallow ponds still worked today to evaporate sea water for salt. The puny species list above belies the importance of this spot for birds. Even though few species are found here regularly, numerous rarities have turned up over the years. Laughing Gulls are found almost every winter, and other rare gulls turn up as well. The mudflats are excellent habitat for migrating shorebirds. It is the kind of place that should always be checked if you are birding in the area. At the small grassy airstrip around the loop from the salt pans, Western Meadowlarks, Northern Mockingbirds, and sometimes great clouds of Chestnut Mannikins can be found.

9. Waimea Canyon

Location: Western Kauai, sweeping inland from the town of Waimea to Kokee.

Access: Follow Kaumualii Highway (Rt. 50) westward to Kekaha. Turn right onto Kokee Rd. (Rt. 55) and head mauka. After about eight miles, you will enter Waimea Canyon State Park. Watch for Waimea Canyon Lookout on the right. From there, continue uphill and look for Puu Hinahina Lookout.

Precautions: Although it looks like a short cut, do not take Waimea Canyon Road (Rt. 550), which is dangerously steep and hazardous, between the town of Waimea and Kokee Road.

Notable Species:	White-tailed Tropicbird	Elepaio
	Erckel's Francolin	**Kauai Amakihi**
	Short-eared Owl	**Apapane**

Waimea Canyon is one of Hawaii's great scenic wonders, the "Grand Canyon of the Pacific." Because the lookouts are all on the west rim, the canyon is best viewed in the afternoon. Thus if you have only a day to spend in the Kokee area, it is best to bypass the canyon lookouts on your way up and stop on your way down. White-tailed Tropicbirds constantly circle on the updrafts in the canyon, and even the casual tourist notices them. Soaring Short-eared Owls are also frequently seen, especially from the lower **Waimea Canyon Lookout**. You will probably also see some feral goats on the barren ridges below. On the rim itself, watch for Erckel's Francolins on the shoulder of the road and around the parking lot at the lower lookout. Apapane are found at both lookouts, but the Elepaio and Kauai Amakihi are seen mostly at **Puu Hinahina** (look in the koa trees between the parking lot and the canyon lookout).

10. Kokee Region

Location: Northwestern Kauai at upper end of Waimea Canyon. Detail Map W.

Access: Take Kokee Road (Rt. 55 to Rt. 550) out of Kekaha. Continue through Waimea Canyon State Park to Kokee State Park. Park Headquarters is on the left in a complex of buildings that includes Kokee Lodge Restaurant and Kokee Natural History Museum (open daily 10 AM to 4 PM). Trail maps and information are available at the museum. A dirt road across from Kokee Lodge is the main access to the more remote roads and trails in the area. Past the headquarters area the main road climbs to Kalalau Valley Lookout. The road turns sharply to the right and continues to its dead end at Puu o Kila Lookout. Rustic but comfortable cabins are available at Kokee Lodge. At certain times, they are very popular so reservations must be made well in advance. For information write Kokee Lodge, P. O. Box 819, Waimea, Kauai, HI 96796 or telephone (808) 335-6061. The restaurant is open for breakfast and lunch daily and for dinner on weekends.

Precautions: Inquire at Kokee Museum about road conditions before taking an ordinary vehicle on the dirt roads east of the paved highway. Keep in mind that while the road may be passable on the way in, it can become impossibly slippery with one quick rain shower. Use discretion and avoid getting stranded miles from help.

Notable Species:

Koloa (Hawaiian Duck)	**Kauai Amakihi**
Erckel's Francolin	Anianiau
Red Junglefowl	Akikiki (Kauai Creeper)
Short-eared Owl	**Akekee**

Elepaio   Iiwi
White-rumped Shama   **Apapane**

The Kokee region, most of which is included in **Kokee State Park**, is by far the best readily accessible locality in the Hawaiian Islands for native forest birds. All of the species listed above except the Akikiki can be found anywhere in the area, although the Akekee may take a little searching. One should also keep in mind the possibility of finding one of Kauai's great rarities such as Kamao or Ou (both recently reported near the intersection of Alakai Swamp and Pihea trails) or even Nukupuu (reported but unconfirmed recently on Puu Ka Ohelo Trail). The view from the two lookouts near the end of the main road is not to be missed, and both spots provide excellent birding. At the **Kalalau Valley Lookout** (photo above), search the small grove of trees around the restrooms for Anianiau, Kauai Amakihi, and Elepaio. Apapane and Anianiau are often seen from the lookout itself. Akekee are not always present but can usually be found in the trees on either side of the road between the parking area and the missile tracking station (the large domed building). At the very end of the road is **Puu o Kila Lookout.** Here, the best birding, surprisingly, is around the parking lot because one can look at eye-level into the tops of ohia trees. Iiwi are more frequent here than at the lower lookout. If you do not find the Akekee at the lookouts, try hiking down the **Pihea Trail**, which begins at Puu o Kila and follows a now-abandoned (fortunately) heavily eroded roadbed along Pihea Ridge. Akekee are always present along Pihea Ridge, and the ever-changing views of Kalalau Valley are a constant source of wonder. The roadbed eventually ends abruptly and the trail becomes at times boggy, at times slippery and steep, but perverse because it gets much better further in. The trail soon bends sharply to the right and drops off the ridge. As it levels out, a new boardwalk, constructed by Hawaiian hiking clubs to protect the fragile bogs from heavy foot traffic, begins. The boardwalk has turned a very challenging and difficult trail into an easy stroll perfect for birding. Akikiki (Kauai Creeper), always quiet and elusive, and Akekee are often seen along the first section of boardwalk, which shortly intersects with the Alakai Swamp Trail, which likewise is now a boardwalk. To the left (onto Alakai Swamp Trail), the boardwalk descends like a huge staircase toward the upper portion of Kawaikoi Stream. The walkway is as yet incomplete near the bottom. Akikiki can be found on either side

of the valley, usually near the stream. Beyond the stream, the trail follows the northern boundary of the Alakai Wilderness Preserve (Kauai 11). The trail eventually reaches a spectacular overlook into Wainiha Valley at Kilohana, but passes through several mucky bogs and becomes increasingly hard to follow the further you go.

Another good area for finding native birds is reached via a complex of

135

roads and trails that heads east from "Rooster Meadow"
at Kokee Museum. The closer parts of these roads are
fairly well maintained and are nearly always passable
for an ordinary vehicle. Take the main road off Kokee
Road and follow it as it descends into a stream valley.
This road is called variously Camp 10 Road or Mohihi
Road. Just before you cross the first bridge, a road
turns left and heads uphill. This short spur takes you
to the Puu Ka Ohelo Trail head. This trail eventually
joins Berry Flat Trail and comes back into Camp 10
Road about a half mile beyond the point where you
started. I find it quicker to go out and back without
making the loop. Crossing the first bridge, the road
heads up a steep hill, which can be very slippery at
times. Once at the top of the hill, the road flattens out
for a while and gets better. You can continue to a
point where the road begins another sharp descent (a

sign here warning "four-wheel-drive only" is badly overgrown and hard to see). There is
room to park on the left before the road descends, and you should do so if you are in an
ordinary car. Unless you have a four-wheel drive, the rest of the trails must be reached on
foot, but the distances are not prohibitive.

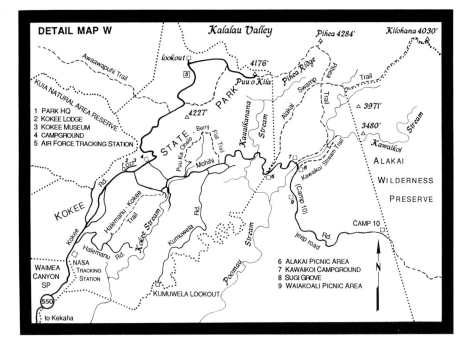

Follow Camp 10 Road on foot until you come to a picnic area on the right in a grassy open area on top of a hill (the inset shows the trail sign at this locality). To the left, before the road descends again, is the **Alakai Swamp Trail**. This trail follows the ridge, soon becoming a boardwalk, and eventually intersects with Pihea Trail discussed earlier. Straight ahead is the "staircase" to Kawaikoi Stream. To the right, Pihea Trail is a spectacularly scenic descent (no boardwalk, but the trail is not bad) to a lower part of Kawaikoi Stream and ends at Camp 10 Road. Just across the stream at this point (there is a concrete ford where you will have to wade) is Sugi Grove, a plantation of Japanese conifers. The Kawaikoi Stream Trail takes off to the left through the trees a short distance uphill from the stream. This is an easy, level train and one of Kokee's most beautiful forest walks. It eventually ends at a fork in the stream. The upper portion is another good place to look for Akikiki. A loop of Alakai Swamp Trail and Pihea Trail plus a walk to the end of Kawaikoi Stream Trail can be accomplished by a good hiker in a day from the new gate on Camp 10 Road.

The Kokee Natural History Museum has exhibits dealing with flora and fauna of the area, and an excellent selection of books for sale. Operated by an organization called Hui o Laka and supported entirely by donations and book sales, it is well worth a visit. Kokee Lodge, a small restaurant and shop next door, sells packets of chicken food you can use if you want a "wild" Red Junglefowl eating out of your hand. These are park-tame birds that have congregated in this area from the surrounding forest to take advantage of the handouts.

11. Alakai Wilderness Preserve

Location: Central Kauai in the roadless area between Kokee and Mt. Waialeale. Detail Map W.

Access: Accessible only by trail. Helicopters are barred from flying over the preserve. Overnight camping is permitted only at Koaie Stream cabin. For camping permits, write to the Division of State Parks (P. O. Box 1671, Lihue, Kauai, HI 96766). The northern end of the preserve is bordered by the Alakai Swamp Trail (see Site 9). The trail to the Koaie Stream cabin in the heart of the Alakai begins at the end of Camp 10 Rd. (4-wheel drive only) at Mohihi. Unfortunately, the only 4WD vehicles available for rent on Kauai are open jeeps with limited space and unreliable performance. An excellent alternative is to hire a local guide with a vehicle. David Kuhn of Terran Tours (P. O. Box 1018, Waimea, HI 96796) is an experienced outfitter who knows the birds well.

Precautions: Hiking in the Alakai wilderness is not for the inexperienced or tender-hearted. The first few miles of trail are well maintained and easy, but the final drop to Koaie Stream is precipitous and difficult. Use flagging tape (be sure to remove it as you return) to mark your route if you stray off obvious trails. Clean your boots before hiking into the Alakai wilderness so as not to exacerbate an already serious problem with alien weeds. Expect to get your feet wet and your clothes muddy.

Notable Species:

Kamao	Nukupuu
Puaiohi	Akikiki (Kauai Creeper)
Elepaio	Akekee
Ou	Iiwi
Kauai Amakihi	Apapane
Anianiau	

This "dream list" of Kauai native birds is really just that. As recently as the early 1980s, one could expect to see at least a few of the rarer birds, but now the prospects are dim. Probably the most likely of the rarer species is the Puaiohi, which was reported along the trail in early 1991. The Kamao is now found only in a tiny, nearly inaccessible area just below the summit of Waialeale. Both the Ou and the Nukupuu could turn up, but both have such low populations that the likelihood of seeing either on a given hike is extremely low. Nevertheless, the hike to the stream cabin (see photo of regulations sign) is worth it just to see a relatively pristine native forest where the more common native birds are abundant and far outnumber the aliens. Of course, a few observers will win the "birding lottery" and see an Ou, Nukupuu, Kamao, or Puaiohi . This area has long been known as the Alakai Swamp, but that is a misnomer. There is no standing water with trees growing in it as in a true swamp. The name was applied because this wet montane forest has numerous bogs and boggy places that are "swampy."

PELAGIC BIRDING

Many kinds of birds can only be seen far from land over the open ocean. The popularity of boat trips to see these pelagic species has greatly increased in recent years, as birders have realized the great potential of such excursions for producing rarities. For reasons that are difficult to understand now, Hawaii for some years had a "bad press" as a place to go birding at sea. Consequently, few observers went out, and little information was available as to what could be seen. We now know that the waters around the Hawaiian Islands are wonderful for birding. On seven pelagic trips in 1989-91 (two from Kauai, 5 from Oahu), I found an average of fifteen bird species including in all but two cases a personal "lifer." That is a major accomplishment for one who has birded in Hawaii since 1974. We are only now beginning to realize the full potential of offshore trips in the islands, and more and more birders are attempting to go out. One advantage that Hawaii has over mainland coasts for pelagic birding is that the deep waters favored by open-ocean species are right offshore. You need go no further than ten miles out to pick up good birds. The islands are mountaintops with no surrounding continental shelf, which also partly explains the near absence of shallow-water feeders such as gulls. The deep channels between the main islands act as funnels for seabirds passing through on a broad front and therefore can be very good birding.

Of course, the majority of the birds seen around the islands are species that breed in Hawaii. Most of the shearwaters will be Wedge-tails, most of the boobies Red-footed and Brown, most of the terns Sooties. Also, the distribution of species at sea reflects the distribution of their nest sites. For example, both albatrosses can be seen near Kauai, but are rare at sea near Oahu; Common Fairy-Terns are frequent off leeward Oahu, but not elsewhere; Gray-backed Terns and Masked Boobies are seen mostly off southeastern Oahu, and Townsend's (Newell's) Shearwaters are mostly around Kauai. All of these species can be seen from land, but seeing them in their more usual habitat at sea is a special experience. A few breeding species (e. g. Bulwer's Petrel, Christmas Shearwater, Band-rumped Storm-Petrel) either cannot be seen from land or are much easier to find from a boat. Among the common birds is always a sprinkling of unusual species that can vary from month to month and even week to week during spring and fall.

Many seabirds that breed in the Southern Hemisphere migrate north during the northern spring and summer. These include a long list of shearwaters and petrels. Recent trips have turned up Sooty Shearwater, Short-tailed Shearwater, Buller's Shearwater, Flesh-footed Shearwater, Juan Fernandez Petrel, Black-winged Petrel, and Mottled Petrel. Another source of rarities are northern breeding seabirds that winter further south. Some of these (e. g. Arctic Tern, Leach's Storm-Petrel, Red Phalarope) only pass through Hawaiian waters in spring or fall, but others (e. g. Pomarine Jaeger, Northern Fulmar) winter in the tropics and may be present October-May. A third source of exciting pelagic species around the main Hawaiian Islands are the Northwestern Hawaiian Islands. Both Bonin Petrel and Tristram's Storm-Petrel were long thought to remain around their nesting islands all year, but both have been recorded recently near the main islands. Obviously, our knowledge of the distribution and movements of seabirds is quite rudimentary. If you go out on your own, be sure to report what you see to the American Birds Regional Editor for Hawaii (currently Dr. Robert L. Pyle, B. P. Bishop Museum, P. O. Box 19000-A, Honolulu HI 96819; 848-4155) so that others can learn from your experience.

One of the ever-present problems with pelagic birding is finding a suitable boat at a reasonable price. Visitors are often surprised that essentially no interisland surface transportation exists in Hawaii. Many small boats cater to tourists, but most are not good for birding for one reason or another. Whale-watching trips from Oahu obviously follow the whales, not the birds, and usually do not go far enough from shore to pick up anything that could not be seen from land. Whale-watching and snorkeling trips into the shallow channel between Lanai and Maui are likewise unproductive. Several operators offer trips along the north shore of Kauai (for details, see the tour desk at any hotel). Some of them use large party boats, while others use rubber Zodiacs. As with the whale-watching boats, these usually do not venture far enough from shore to do the birder much good.

Deep-sea sport-fishing boats provide the best birding. Fishermen in Hawaiian waters have learned that the schools of fish that attract seabirds also attract tuna, so they use the wheeling flocks of boobies, which can be seen from far off, to find the fish. You will not feel slighted if you join a fishing party for birding. The booby flocks attract other seabirds as well as fishermen, and as you approach you will usually see shearwaters, petrels, and terns feeding below the boobies. Most of the party boats are small, limited to six passengers. You can expect to pay $100 or more for a few hours on the water, whether you fish or not. The smaller boats are also relatively unstable and thus less desirable for birding. Most hotels have a display of brochures that advertise the varied fishing options. Sport fishing operations are concentrated in Kona on the Big Island, the south coast of Kauai (Lihue and Port Allen), and Honolulu.

Large party boats, such as are common on the mainland, are scarce in Hawaii. I know of none presently operating out of Kauai or Kona, but two excellent boats are available from Honolulu: the *Golden Eagle* and the *Kono* (P. O. Box 22012, Honolulu HI 96822; 531-4966). Both are large and stable, with covered flying bridges. Both offer special rates for non-fishing riders. The two are berthed next to each other in the middle of the front row (parallel to the street) at Kewalo Boat Harbor along Ala Moana Boulevard between downtown and Ala Moana Shopping Center. Typically, their "all-day" trips depart at 6:30 AM and return about 3 PM. The only problem is that they go out only if they have enough customers, and the best seasons for birds are the low seasons for tourism. You may not know until the last minute whether a trip will go. The only way to be sure you can go on a given day is to charter the boat. Charters for an eight-hour trip currently run about $600 for up to six people, with an additional charge (usually under $60) for each passenger over six. Thus a party of ten could charter the boat for about $80 apiece. These prices do not include any food or beverages, which can be provided by the boats for an additional charge.

Organized birding tours sometimes include a pelagic charter, and usually open the trip to local birders and any others interested. The cost varies with the number of participants. Both of the boats mentioned above can take up to thirty, so space is not a problem. For news of upcoming organized birding charters, contact Hawaii Audubon Society (212 Merchant St., Rm. 320, Honolulu HI 96813; (808) 528-1432). They usually will know about any trips sponsored by private tour groups.

In Hawaii as elsewhere, pelagic birding has its own special problems. If you are susceptible to seasickness, take the necessary precautions. Hawaiian waters are not as cold as those off mainland coasts, but you should still be prepared for cooler temperatures than you experience on land. The tropical sun is particularly intense on the water, so sunscreens are essential. Be sure to have some protection from salt spray for your binoculars and wipe them thoroughly after you return. If you wear a hat, be sure to tether it around your neck or you are sure to lose it to the wind.

THE SPECIES GUIDE

This section is **not** a complete species list; it includes only those species that are of special interest for one reason or another. All endemic or indigenous breeding birds are included. Localities from The Site Guide are referred to by island name and number (i. e. "Maui 6" or "Oahu 3"). Complete directions are given here for the few localities not covered in The Site Guide.

Pied-billed Grebe. This species was long considered only a rare straggler to the Hawaiian Islands, but in the early 1980s it colonized Aimakapa Pond (Hawaii 6) as a breeding resident. This population, which is thriving and apparently increasing yearly, thus represents one of the few natural island colonizations to be witnessed by ornithologists. Pied-billed Grebes still show up as stragglers on other islands and on other ponds on the Big Island, but now no one knows whether they represent visitors from the mainland or wanderers from the Aimakapa colony.

Black-footed Albatross. Although this species breeds in great numbers in the Northwestern Hawaiian Islands, it is strictly pelagic around the main islands and can be rather elusive. Most sightings are near Kauai and Oahu. These albatrosses can sometimes be seen from land, particularly from promontories such as Makahuena Point (Kauai 6). They have also been seen occasionally off Sand Island (Oahu 17). In the

spring, Black-foots sometimes visit the Laysan Albatross colony at Kilauea Point (Kauai 2), but so far none has taken up residence. The best way to see a Black-footed Albatross is to take a boat offshore from either Kauai or Oahu. Kauai is better because it is closer to the nearest breeding colonies on islets off Niihau. For information about boats, see the section on Offshore Birding.

Laysan Albatross. This albatross is much easier to see around the
main Hawaiian Islands than the previous
one. The best place is Kilauea Point
(Kauai 2), where several dozen pairs are
now breeding. The birds are present most
of the year, but are absent from late summer
to late fall. A few early arrivals will show
up in November. On Oahu, Laysan Albatrosses have attempted to nest at sev-

eral spots, but have never succeeded because of the presence of so many ground
predators (mongooses, dogs, cats, etc.). During the first half of the year, a few pairs can
often be found on the ground at Dillingham Airfield west of Waialua (Oahu 14). To
reach the area from Honolulu, take H-2 north to its terminus at Schofield Barracks and
continue ahead on Rt. 803. Dillingham is beyond the town of Waialua on 803. The
landing strip parallels the highway on the mauka side, and this is where the birds usually
rest. Several openings in the vegetation along the fence provide vantage points from
which to search. Other places to look include Mokuleia Beach Park and the polo
grounds on the makai side of the road. Laysan Albatrosses can be seen in flight
anywhere along Oahu's North Shore (Oahu 13), but are unpredictable at any given
locality.

Hawaiian (Dark-rumped) Petrel. This Endangered Species breeds only in the
Galapagos and Hawaiian islands, and recent research indicates that the two populations
may be distinct species. So even if you have seen the Galapagos birds, you should try to
see the Hawaiian ones if you have the opportunity. The main Hawaiian colony is in the
rocky walls of Haleakala Crater (Maui 4), but smaller colonies apparently exist on other
islands. The birds spend the nonbreeding months (November-February) far at sea and are
seldom seen. At the end of February, they return to the colony at night to prepare their
burrows for nesting. Nonbreeding birds also congregate and fly about over the colony.
From March until mid-August their calls can be heard on any calm night. Seeing them
requires good ears for direction and a strong spotlight. The colony is just below the visitor
center at the crater overlook. Petrels can be heard from the visitor center itself, but a better
place is a short distance below it. Drive to the parking area, then head back down the road
until you see the first road sign. The shoulder just before the sign is wide enough for you
to park your car completely off the pavement (which is recommended). The crater rim
here is only a few yards to the right through jagged boulders and volcanic gravel (watch
your step; it can be treacherous). From the rim one can, on a good night, hear petrels
calling beginning about an hour after sunset. Calling reaches a peak two or three hours
later and tapers off after midnight. Getting a spotlight beam on a flying bird can be a
challenge, but occasionally one will be attracted to the light and actually land right at your
feet! Although pairs with chicks continue to use the colony after mid-August (fledging
is in October), they are not very vocal and seeing one is rather difficult.

In the fall, when young birds are fledging, many are disoriented by artificial lighting and become grounded on lawns and in parking lots. Most years a few Hawaiian Petrels are turned in among the much more frequently grounded Townsend's Shearwaters on Kauai, but the petrels are more often picked up on Maui, as one might expect. For a more detailed discussion of this phenomenon, see the Townsend's Shearwater account below.

Another way to see a Hawaiian Petrel is to observe one at sea during the day. The best time for this is during April, when breeding birds stay away from the colonies to fortify themselves for the coming incubation period. At this time, with the aid of a good telescope, one can sometimes see them from land. A particularly good place to look is Makahuena Point (Kauai 6) at dusk. The petrels can be distinguished from the much more numerous Townsend's Shearwaters by their larger size, different manner of flight, and lack of obvious white sides to the rump from above.

Bonin Petrel. This species breeds in the Northwestern Hawaiian Islands and until recently was considered very rare near the main islands. Recent fall sightings off Oahu indicate that Bonin Petrels may be more common as postbreeding visitors around the main islands than previously believed. Look for them on pelagic trips off Oahu and Kauai in October and November.

Mottled Petrel. This is one of the most frequently reported of the migratory gadfly-petrels that visit Hawaiian waters. It has been seen most frequently off Oahu, but that may reflect the distribution of observers more than the distribution of birds. The best months to look for Mottled Petrels are March-April and October-November. See Offshore Birding for information about boats.

Bulwer's Petrel. This species breeds in low numbers on many offshore islets near the main Hawaiian Islands including Moku Manu (Oahu 8), Manana (Oahu 6), Molokini (Maui 9), and Lehua off the northern tip of Niihau. They are frequently seen on pelagic trips into waters off Oahu and Kauai and occasionally off the Kona Coast of the Big Island. For information about boat trips, see Offshore Birding. Unfortunately, the birds come and go from their nests at night and are seldom seen from shore. Two places to look for this species with a good spotting scope are Makahuena Point (Kauai 6) and the southern Kihei area on Maui, directly opposite Molokini (Maui 9).

Wedge-tailed Shearwater. This is the common breeding shearwater in the Hawaiian Islands. Probably nine out of ten shearwaters observed on pelagic trips into Hawaiian waters are Wedge-tails. They are hard to miss. They nest on rocky promontories and offshore islets where they come and go during daylight. Wedge-tails are thus easily seen from land. At Kilauea Point (Kauai 2), one can approach birds on the  ground very closely. Good places to look for them from land include Laie Point (Oahu 10), Koko Head (Oahu 5), Makapuu (Oahu 6), Molokini Islet (Maui 7), South Point (Hawaii 3), and Makahuena Point (Kauai 6).

Christmas Shearwater. This species nests in low numbers on Moku Manu (Oahu 8) and Lehua Islet off the northern tip of Niihau. Christmas Shearwaters can be seen off southern Kauai and windward Oahu, but are less common than the migratory Sooty Shearwater with which they could easily be confused. They are rarely seen from land, but with patience an observer can pick a few out from the numerous Wedge-tails flying past Koko Head (Oahu 5) or Laie Point (Oahu 10) late in the day during spring.

Townsend's (Newell's) Shearwater. In most literature on Hawaiian birds, this species is called Newell's Shearwater, but that name applies properly only to the local subspecies. Townsend's Shearwaters nest in burrows high in the mountains of several of the Hawaiian Islands, but mostly on Kauai and Oahu. Between April and October, adult birds are commonly seen on pelagic trips near Kauai and less frequently off Oahu. They can be seen from shore at dusk with the aid of a spotting scope at several places around Kauai including Haena (Kauai 4), Kapaa, and Makahuena Point (Kauai 7). Late in the day hundreds of shearwaters begin staging offshore where they form huge swirling flocks low over the water. From time to time, one bird will begin to spiral upward from the flock and upon reaching the desired altitude will fly in a beeline from the sea toward the mountains, passing high overhead. Adults scatter after mid-October, just before the young fledge. During October and November, young birds disoriented by the lights of towns and resorts sometimes are grounded in numbers on highways and lawns. They should be looked for in parking lots and

on lawns near bright lights particularly after cloudy or moonless nights. The vicinity of Kapaa on the east coast and Poipu on the south seem to be "hot spots" for such groundings, but the birds can be found anywhere around the island. If you find a grounded bird, you should take it to the nearest fire station where special boxes are available to hold the birds until they can be rehabilitated and released. In Kapaa, the station is just north of and across the main highway from the Sheraton Coconut Beach Hotel. In Poipu, birds should be taken to Koloa, where the fire station is on the right as you head for Lihue. Grounded birds may appear injured (shearwaters' legs are so far back that they cannot walk well on land, and they cannot take off from level ground) but usually are perfectly well unless they have been hit by cars or attacked by pets. Be sure to point both head and tail away from clothing that could be soiled; shearwaters can squirt from both ends!

Tristram's (Sooty) Storm-Petrel. As far as anyone knows at present, this species breeds only in the uninhabited Northwestern Hawaiian Islands, and is seen at sea only around the nesting islands. Recently, however, a fledgling was picked up alive at Hilo Harbor. Whether this bird represents an unknown breeding colony in the main islands or rode to Hilo on a fishing boat is not known. Birders on pelagic trips near the main islands should not totally rule out the possibility of seeing this species.

White-tailed Tropicbird. White-tailed Tropicbirds are most easily seen on Kauai where they are present year-round and can be seen virtually anywhere. Any valley or canyon with steep-walled sides may have them. White-tailed Tropicbirds are more seasonal on other islands and may be hard to find during the winter months. They are always scarce on Oahu, but are occasionally seen along the windward coast. On Maui, look for them in Haleakala Crater (Maui 4) and Iao Valley (Maui 3). On the Big Island, the most reliable spot is Halemaumau in Kilauea Crater (Hawaii 2). The birds nest in the walls of the "fire-pit" despite the heavy sulfurous fumes and can usually be seen circling about. Other good places to look for them include Honuapo Bay at Whittington Beach Park between Naalehu and Pahala, Hilo Bay, and Waipio Valley.

Red-tailed Tropicbird. This species is more restricted in its distribution than the previous one, and is much more seasonal. Even though the birds remain near the islands during the winter, they are scattered and seldom seen. The best place for excellent views of Red-tails is Kilauea Point (Kauai 2), where they cavort in their somersaulting aerial displays right at eye level. On Oahu, they are often seen near Koko Crater just inland from the Halona Blowhole overlook (Oahu 5), and near Manana

Island (Oahu 6). At the latter site, the best place to view them is the upper lookout above Makapuu Beach. The only other place that this species is regularly reported is along the eastern side of Lanai, which is visited by some organized snorkeling excursions out of Lahaina, Maui.

Masked Booby. This is the rarest of the three Hawaiian boobies and is regularly found in the main islands only off southeastern Oahu. A few pairs nest on Moku Manu (Oahu 8) and can be identified through a spotting scope from Ulupau Head. Look for them along the crest of the island. Masked Boobies have been seen flying past Laie Point (Oahu 10) on a few occasions, and from boats cruising off Makapuu Point and Diamond Head.

Brown Booby. Although fairly common, Brown Boobies are much more localized in their distribution than the abundant Red-foots. They will turn up on almost any pelagic trip, but are not so easily seen from land except in a few places. They are frequent along the windward coast of Oahu and nest on Moku Manu (Oahu 8). They are frequently seen at Makapuu (Oahu 6) and Laie Point (Oahu 10). On Kauai, the best place to look is Kilauea Point (Kauai 2), but Brown Boobies can be anywhere along the north shore. Haena Beach (Kauai 4) is particularly good. Elsewhere on Kauai, the birds are mostly seen flying far offshore. They can usually be seen from Makahuena Point (Kauai 6). This species is less often seen on islands south of Oahu, but are sometimes seen from South Point (Hawaii 3).

Red-footed Booby. This is the abundant booby in Hawaii. However, to get a close look at a perched bird, one must visit one of the breeding colonies. Because they nest in trees, Red-footed Boobies can maintain colonies on the main islands despite the presence of predators such as mongooses, dogs, and cats that preclude nesting by other seabirds that nest on the ground. The two main colonies are in Ulupau Crater (Oahu 7) and at Kilauea Point (Kauai 2). The Kauai colony is more readily accessible, but you can get closer to nesting birds on Oahu.

Great Frigatebird. Frigatebirds can be seen virtually anywhere around Kauai and Oahu, but are much less common elsewhere. On Oahu, particularly good places to see them include Waikiki (Oahu 3), Makapuu (Oahu 6), the Kaneohe/Kailua area (Oahu 7-8), and along the North Shore (Oahu 14). On Kauai, the best place is Kilauea Point (Kauai 2).

Fulvous Whistling-Duck. This species first appeared in Hawaii in 1982 and since then has nested every year and built up a small population on Oahu. Whether these birds were illegally introduced or colonized the island naturally may never be known. The species is undergoing a worldwide range expansion, so natural colonization is at least plausible. The birds can be seen easily at Amorient Aquafarm and Kii Pond (Oahu 11).

Nene (Hawaiian Goose). Hawaii's state bird had nearly become extinct by the 1940s, but a worldwide effort at captive breeding and reintroduction has brought it back from the brink. Historically known only from the Big Island (but now known to have inhabited the other islands in prehistoric times), the Nene has been reintroduced to Maui and Kauai. Probably the easiest place to see one is Haleakala National Park (Maui 4) where a few park-tame wild birds sometimes hang around the visitor center at park headquarters. Hikers often encounter Nene in the grassy eastern end of Haleakala Crater. On Hawaii, the best place to see them is around Kilauea Crater in Hawaii Volcanoes NP (Hawaii 2), particularly near Waldron Ledge and Keanakakoi Crater. Surprisingly, the Kipuka Ainahou Nene Sanctuary on the Saddle Road is not a reliable place to see the birds, at least from the highway. Recently, a flock has been seen regularly in the vicinity of Puu Anahulu (Hawaii 8), especially in the new Puu Lani Ranch subdivision. The Kauai birds are not yet "countable" because they are not known to be successfully established. Birds that originated from escapees have been seen around the Westin Kauai Resort golf course in Lihue. More recent introductions have been made at Kilauea Point (Kauai 2).

Koloa (Hawaiian Duck). This Hawaiian endemic survived as a natural population only on Kauai, but it has been reintroduced on Oahu and Hawaii. On Kauai, Koloa can be found on almost any pond or reservoir and are sometimes seen along forest streams in the mountains. The best place to see them in numbers is Hanalei NWR (Kauai 3). Another frequently visited spot that almost always has a few Koloa is Alakoko Pond in Huleia Valley (Kauai 5). The easiest place to see them on Oahu is the Kahuku area (Oahu 11-12), but they can also be found in Waialua (Oahu 14) and around Pearl Harbor (Oahu 15). Koloa are rather scarce on the Big Island and are not often seen on the ponds most frequently visited by birders. They are more likely to be found on ranch reservoirs along Keanakolu Road on the way to Hakalau Forest NWR (Hawaii 14) or on the more accessible Mana Road pond near Waimea (Hawaii 9).

Hawaiian Hawk. Found only on the Big Island, the often elusive native hawk can be seen virtually anywhere on the island, even over canefields or in the Hilo suburbs,

but is unpredictable at any given locality. If you spend enough time birding on Hawaii, you should see it eventually. One of the most consistently reliable spots for the hawk is Stainback Hwy. near Hilo. To reach it, take Rt 11 (Hawaii Belt Rd.) out of Hilo toward Volcano and look for a right turn to Kulani. Turn here and proceed mauka. The hawks can be anywhere along this road and often sit in

dead snags. About seven miles from the turn-off, you must turn left onto Kulani Road (Stainback Hwy is closed to the public above this point) which will reconnect with Rt 11 at Mountain View. To approach Stainback Highway from the direction of Hawaii Volcanoes NP, proceed toward Hilo and look for a left turn marked "Kulani 17" in Mountain View village. Take this road about four miles to Stainback Highway where you must turn right. If you strike out on Stainback Highway, other good spots to try include the village of Volcano near the national park, Mauna Loa Road in the park (Hawaii 2), Rt 11 in South Kona between Manuka SP (Hawaii 4) and Kealakekua (Hawaii 5), Kaloko Mauka Subdivision (Hawaii 7), and ravines along the Hamakua Coast north of Hilo.

Black Francolin. Although introduced on several islands, this species is most easily found in the drier parts of the Big Island. Look for them along highways in South Kohala. A recent "hot spot" has been the new Puu Lani Ranch subdivision at Puu Anahulu (Hawaii 8), where Black Francolins can be seen foraging along the roadside especially late in the afternoon. Another good place to look is along Waikoloa Road. On Maui, listen for their calls in cane fields just below Pukalani and along Hansen Road.

Erckel's Francolin. Of the francolins, this is the one most likely to be in or near forests. On Kauai, it is often seen along the highway from Waimea Canyon (Kauai 8) to Kokee (Kauai 9). Some have become "park tame" and hang around the parking lot at Waimea Canyon Overlook. On the Big Island, they are most common in North Kona, South Kohala, and in areas along the Saddle Road. Look for them along Mamalahoa Highway (Rt 190) between Kalaoa and Huehue Ranch and at Puu Anahulu. On the Saddle Road, they are often seen in the vicinity of Waikii Ranch and at Puu Laau (Hawaii 9).

Gray Francolin. Gray Francolins are most readily seen on Maui and Hawaii, although they are present on other islands. They have been seen regularly in recent years in Na Laau Arboretum on the slopes of Diamond Head (Oahu 3). They are very common in the Maui lowlands and can turn up on the shoulder of the road almost anywhere. They are attracted to water sources and are often found on lawns in the Kihei/Wailea area (a particularly good spot is the Maui Lu Resort). On the Big Island, they are widespread in dry habitats and as on Maui are drawn to irrigated lawns and golf courses. They can be seen close at hand around homes in the village of Waikoloa, and are usually present at Puu Kohola Heiau NHS (Hawaii 10) below the lower heiau. They also inhabit resort golf courses with clumps of kiawe trees along the Kohala Coast south of Kawaihae.

Chukar. Although Chukars are frequently seen in dry parts of the Big Island, they are unpredictable at any given spot. They are usually present on the Waimea Plains (Hawaii 9), especially on the road behind the cement plant. On Maui, by far the best place to see them is between the lower visitor center and the summit area in Haleakala National Park (Maui 4). A particularly good spot is around the silversword enclosure at Kalahaku Overlook. The best time of day to find them close to the road is late afternoon, when most park visitors have gone home.

Japanese Quail. This small quail is very elusive in Hawaii. I have personally seen them only on Kauai, although I have heard them on a few occasions on the Big Island. The problem is that they like grassy fields where the grass is under about 5 in. high. Thus a freshly mowed field that is good for them one year may have grown up and be unproductive the next and regularly grazed fields may be  too closely cropped. On Kauai, the most reliable area in which to search for them is the northeastern part of the island between Anahola and Kilauea. On Hawaii, they have been reported recently in ranch lands along Keanakolu Rd. above Hakalau Forest NWR (Hawaii 11). The birds call mostly very early in the morning in spring and summer. Look for fields with grass of the proper height, then listen for the sneezy calls. Once you have located a field with calling birds, you can try walking through it to flush the birds into view. They are virtually impossible to see on the ground, and allow fairly close approach before they fly.

*Kalij Pheasant. This species is becoming increasingly common on Hawaii, the only island where it occurs. They can turn up almost anywhere and are usually shy, but in a few places have become rather tame and allow close approach. Probably the best place is the Mauna Loa Rd., including Kipuka Puaulu, in Hawaii Volcanoes NP (Hawaii 2). Other good localities include Kaloko Mauka Subdivision (Hawaii 7), Puu Anahulu (Hawaii 8), and Hakalau Forest NWR (Hawaii 11).

Red Junglefowl. These feral chickens, descendants of birds brought to the islands by the first Hawaiians, survive only on Kauai where they can be found almost anywhere. The problem is differentiating between true wild junglefowl and domestic chickens. Nowadays, most domestic stock is kept penned so any wild-looking chicken seen along the roadside is a potential Red Junglefowl. Most domestic chickens have bright golden yellow legs, whereas true junglefowl have legs that range from dark gray to yellowish pink. Anyone who likes these birds should not miss the spectacle of the park-tame birds that beg for handouts around Kokee Lodge and Museum (Kauai 10). All chickens at Kokee are believed to be true Red Junglefowl, although recently a fair number of odd plumage variations have been turning up there.

Common Peafowl. Peafowl were introduced to the Hawaiian Islands over a century ago but are still of rather local distribution. The best place to see them is in North Kona on the Big Island. The birds can be seen in stone-walled pastures above and below the Mamalahoa Highway (Rt. 190) between Kalaoa and Huehue Ranch (Mileposts 30-32). The ranch entrance is marked with a large arching sign on the mauka side of the highway. The peafowl inhabit the groves of silk oak and jacaranda but are often seen in the open as well. Early in the morning look for them perched in trees on the steep hillside north of the ranch entrance. Peafowl are also present at Puu Anahulu (Hawaii 8) south of the highway and east of Puu Lani Ranch, but these may be domesticated birds.

Wild Turkey. Wild Turkeys are fairly common and easy to see in parts of the Big Island, including the locality mentioned for Common Peafowl. They should also be looked for along the lower part of the Waimea (northern) end of the Saddle Road. They are hard to miss on the road to Puu Laau (Hawaii 11). Another good place to look is along the lower part of the Mauna Kea Road (the only major paved road heading toward Mauna Kea from the Saddle Road).

Gambel's Quail. This quail is uncommon and elusive on the southern slopes of Mauna Kea on the Big Island. It forms mixed coveys with California Quail, so can be difficult to pick out. Look for it in rocky places along the Keanakolu Road between

Mauna Kea Road and Hakalau Forest NWR (Hawaii 14). It is the only quail on Kahoolawe (which is off-limits) and is said to be well established on Lanai, but I have no specific directions for finding it there.

California Quail. California Quail are found mostly in the Saddle area of the Big Island and in Hawaii Volcanoes NP. Look for them at Waikii Ranch and in the picnic grounds at Pohakuloa (Hawaii 12). They are hard to miss on the road to Puu Laau (Hawaii 11). Look for them also on the Mauna Loa Road in the national park (Hawaii 2), especially late in the day when they may be sitting in the road. Another good spot is Volcano Golf Course, just outside the park across Rt 11 from Kilauea Military Camp. California Quail populations appear to be cyclic, and some years they can be very hard to find even in reliable spots.

Common Moorhen. Moorhens in Hawaii belong to an endemic endangered subspecies. They are found in habitat typical for the species, which is rare in the islands. Today, they are found only on Kauai, Oahu, and Molokai. Good places to see them include Hanalei NWR (Kauai 3), the Wailua Flats (Kauai 1), Kawainui Marsh (Oahu 6), James Campbell NWR (Oahu 11-12), the Waialua lotus ponds (Oahu 14), and Kakahaia NWR (Molokai 1).

Hawaiian Coot. Probably the most common of Hawaii's endangered freshwater birds, coots can be expected on virtually any body of water, including estuaries. All the localities mentioned for the Common Moorhen are good for coots as well, but coots are also found on Maui and Hawaii and on ponds that have no habitat for moorhens. Look for them on Kanaha (Maui 1) and Kealia (Maui 2) ponds on Maui. On the Big Island, good spots include the Hilo ponds (Hawaii 1), Mana Road pond (Hawaii 13), and Aimakapa Pond (Hawaii 6). Coots will be on almost any body of water on Kauai. [Note: The Hawaiian Coot was considered a subspecies of American Coot by the 1983 AOU Check-list. A 1987 paper by the author presented reasons for considering it a separate species. The check-list committee has not yet acted on the recommendation, but other references have recognized the Hawaiian Coot as a full species.] Not all coots seen in the Hawaiian Islands belong to the local form. Mainland American Coots turn up in very low numbers some winters, mixed in with the local birds. Consult *A Field Guide to the Birds of Hawaii and the Tropical Pacific* for field marks that distinguish the two. For illustration, see Figure 4.

Pacific Golden-Plover. No birder in Hawaii from August through April needs to be told where to find this ubiquitous species. Even during the summer, a few nonbreeding birds remain behind in the islands. Oversummering birds tend to be found in wetland habitats rather than parks and lawns. Wintering birds often are territorial, with the same individual found daily in the same small area for months. An interesting activity is to watch one of these birds as it changes gradually from the drab nonbreeding plumage into its bright breeding dress. In the spring, such freshly plumaged birds gather in staging areas, sometimes by the hundreds, before their northward migration. Notable staging grounds include Kualoa Regional Park (Oahu 9) and pastures high on the southern slope of Mauna Kea along Keanakolu Road (see Hawaii 14).

Black-necked Stilt. Like the moorhen, the stilt of Hawaii is an endemic endangered subspecies. Although they number at most a few thousand individuals, they are conspicuous and can be found in any wetland, including temporary rain pools. Nesting habitat that is secure from ground predators such as mongooses is, however, severely limited. The most accessible places to see them include Amorient Aquafarm (Oahu 11), Hanalei NWR (Kauai 3), Hanapepe Salt Pans (Kauai 8), and Kanaha Pond (Maui 1).

Bristle-thighed Curlew. This large shorebird, which nests in Alaska, is a common winter visitor to the Northwestern Hawaiian Islands, but is mostly a rare passage migrant in the main islands. One of the most reliable localities for Bristle-thighed Curlews is the Kahuku area (Oahu 11-12). During August and September, a few are almost always in a pasture that lies between James Campbell NWR (Oahu 11) and the beach. Occasionally, an individual will remain here through the winter. A good vantage point from which to scope this area is a small Oriental cemetery at the north end of the golf course in the village of Kahuku. To reach it, take Puuluana Street makai across from Kahuku School. At the clubhouse, turn left and follow the sand road as it skirts the golf course. You will have to do this on foot if the gate is closed. It is possible to walk through the pasture, but it is private land so ask permission if anyone is around. Another seemingly ideal, but less reliable, place to look is South Point (Hawaii 3).

155

Sharp-tailed Sandpiper. Rare on the mainland, this is one of the more common spring and fall transient shorebirds in Hawaii. Good places to look for this species, as well as Pectoral Sandpipers and peeps, include Hanalei NWR (Kauai 5), Waita Reservoir (Kauai 7), James Campbell NWR (Oahu 11), Honouliuli Unit of Pearl Harbor NWR (Oahu 16), Kanaha and Kealia ponds (Maui 1-2), and Aimakapa Pond (Hawaii 6). The peaks of migration for small shorebirds in Hawaii are usually in April and October.

Pomarine Jaeger. Although mostly pelagic, these winter visitors to Hawaii tend to congregate just outside Honolulu Harbor. Probably the best place to see one from shore is Sand Island (Oahu 18). They can be identified at great distance by the continuously flapping, high-off-the-water flight and dark plumage. The Pomarine Jaeger is often the first "good" bird encountered on boat trips that leave from Kewalo Basin.

Gray-backed Tern. This species is found mostly in the uninhabited Northwestern Hawaiian Islands but can be seen at sea south of Kauai and off southeastern Oahu. A large colony nests on Moku Manu (Oahu 8) and the birds can be seen with difficulty through a spotting scope from Ulupau Head. Look for them on the ground among Sooty Terns at the upper right "corner" of the  island. Their paler color, smaller size, and white collar help to distinguish them from Sooties in the swirling flocks of terns over the island. Some years, at least, the Gray-backs remain at the colony several weeks after the Sooties have departed. Gray-backs can sometimes be seen offshore with the aid of a spotting scope. Two particularly good places to watch for them are the lookouts near the Diamond Head lighthouse and Koko Head Regional Park (Oahu 5).

Sooty Tern. The primary nesting colonies for this common pantropical tern in Hawaii are on Moku Manu (Oahu 8) and Manana Island (Oahu 6). At these sites they form great clouds of birds between April and September, but during the rest of the year they are strictly pelagic.

Brown Noddy. This common dark tern can be seen at sea anywhere around the Hawaiian Islands, but is seen from land most often around Oahu and Kauai. It nests on offshore islands rather than coastal cliffs and tends to be solitary. Noddies in flocks of more than three usually are Blacks.

Black Noddy. This species is much more localized than the common and widespread Brown Noddy. On Kauai, they nest in cliffs along the Na Pali Coast, where they are most easily seen from the sightseeing craft that visit this area. The best land-based place to see them is Kee Beach (Kauai 4). On Oahu, look for them in flight over Nuupia Pond (Oahu 8) or perched in tight clusters on the beaches of Manana Island (Oahu 6). An excellent place to compare the two noddies against a dark sea background is Ulupau Head at the tip of Mokapu Peninsula. On Maui, the best place to find them is Waianapanapa Caves SP near Hana, while on the Big Island they are most easily found below the cliffs of the coastal section of Hawaii Volcanoes NP (Hawaii 2). A particularly good spot is the Holei Sea Arch.

Common Fairy-Tern. These beautiful and popular birds occur only on Oahu in the main Hawaiian Islands . They might well be considered urban birds because they are found almost entirely in and around Honolulu. They feed offshore during the middle of the day, so are most often observed over land in the morning and late afternoon. One of the most reliable places to see fairy-terns in flight is, surprisingly, the Hawaii State Capitol. For birds on eggs or tending young, the best place is Kapiolani Park in Waikiki (Oahu 3). At the other end of Waikiki, look for them in the big trees between the Hale Koa Hotel at Fort DeRussy and the beach and around the Hilton Hawaiian Village Hotel, especially the small park on the southeast corner of Ala Moana Boulevard and Kalia Road.

Chestnut-bellied Sandgrouse. In Hawaii, this species is found only in the Waimea Plains (Hawaii 9). Flocks often fly over the Mamalahoa Highway (Hawaii Belt Rd., Rt. 190) between Waimea and the Saddle Road early in the morning or in late afternoon. Two particularly good spots are near the Waimea-Kohala Airport and at the West Hawaii Concrete plant near the Saddle
Road intersection. A paved road to the concrete plant continues through extensive pastures where sandgrouse are often found on the ground. The road is open from 7 AM to 3 PM and sometimes later (after 3, be careful not to get locked in.) Sandgrouse flocks wander widely, so they could be encountered anywhere in the South Kohala-North Kona region.

Mourning Dove. The only one of the four dove species in Hawaii that is difficult to find, the Mourning Dove is confined to the Big Island. Most recent sightings have been in the South Kohala District. Look for it at Puu Lani Ranch subdivision (Hawaii 8) and along Waikoloa Road, especially the upper end. By far the most reliable locality is Kawaihae, where doves of all species gather to feed on waste grain and pick up grit at the harbor. As you approach the harbor complex from the south, look for several huge white storage tanks on the left, with a flat paved area between them and the highway. On weekdays, you can drive in among the piles of sand or grain, but at any time Mourning Doves can be seen from the main highway among the other species.

Rose-ringed Parakeet. The most reliable place to see this species is in the Hanapepe-Kalaheo area (Kauai 8). The parakeets are a pest in corn fields in lower Hanapepe Valley during spring and early summer. They formerly roosted in trees at the edge of the golf course in Kukuiolono Park in Kalaheo (and may still be there occasionally), but their present roost site is unknown to me. They are often seen in Kalaheo in the early morning flying from somewhere makai of the town. An observer parked along the highway west of town in the early morning should see them high overhead. Another good vantage point is the Hanapepe Valley overlook on Hwy. 50 between Kalaheo and Eleele. Here, they may be seen flying up the valley or perched in trees below. Parakeets have been reported recently feeding during midday at Olu Pua Gardens (look for sign on the right just past Kalaheo). Rose-ringed Parakeets are much more elusive on Oahu. Look for them in ironwood trees in Kapiolani Park or along the trail to Na Laau Arboretum (Oahu 3) where they may have a roost. In the Kona area of the Big Island, a roost has been reported above the town of Kainaliu between Honalo and Kealakekua, but its usage appears to be irregular.

Barn Owl. Although widespread, this introduced owl can be elusive. It is much more nocturnal than the Short-eared Owl, and the two seem to operate different "shifts" at some localities. One of the most reliable spots is Kilauea Point (Kauai 2) and the surrounding open fields on the north shore of Kauai. Look for them also in the Koloa-Poipu area in the southern part of the island. On the Big Island, Barn Owls have been seen recently at Puu Anahulu (Hawaii 8).

Short-eared Owl. The native owl is found on all islands but is most easily seen on Kauai, Maui, and Hawaii. On the Big Island, they are common along the northern half of the Saddle Road (Rt. 200) where they soar over pastures and perch on fence posts, where they often allow close approach. They are also often seen around Waimea (Hawaii 9), at Puu Anahulu (Hawaii 8), and along the road to South Point (Hawaii 3). On Maui, they are most numerous in the pasturelands on the lower slopes of Haleakala, particularly between Pukalani and Haleakala NP (Maui 4). The *pueo*, as it is known locally, is found all over Kauai and can turn up almost anywhere. Look for them along the highway between Kalaheo and Hanapepe. Soaring owls are often seen from the lower Waimea Canyon overlook (Kauai 9).

Island Swiftlet. The only known nesting colony of this endangered species, introduced to Oahu from Guam, is in North Halawa Valley. Unfortunately, the valley is now off-limits to birders because it is being destroyed by construction of the H-3 freeway. Congress, over the bitter objections of environmental groups, granted this project an exemption from the Endangered Species Act (primarily so the builders would not have to be concerned about the Oahu Creeper). One wonders what good the Act is if projects can be arbitrarily exempted. Perhaps, if the swiftlets survive the construction, future birders will see them flying over the freeway.

Eurasian Skylark. These are birds of open country mostly on Maui and Hawaii. One can hardly stop anywhere in the lower to mid-elevation ranch lands on Haleakala without hearing their incredibly long and complex songs. They often rest on grassy shoulders of the road and fly up when cars approach. On the Big Island, they are abundant in open pastures along the Saddle Road (Rt. 200) and Mana-Keanakolu Road that encircles the windward side of Mauna Kea. They may also be easily found at South Point (Hawaii 3) and around Kilauea Crater in Hawaii Volcanoes NP (Hawaii 2).

Hawaiian Crow. Birders now have almost no chance of seeing this critically endangered species in the wild. The tiny captive flock, probably the species' only chance for long-term survival, is housed in the state breeding facility at Olinda, Maui where efforts to build up their numbers are hampered by senility and inbreeding. The State of Hawaii has set up a crow sanctuary on Hualalai, but there are no crows in it. The last remaining wild flock (under twenty birds) lives on the McCandless Ranch in South Kona, Hawaii, where the ranch owners are doing everything possible to prevent the taking of additional birds from the wild to bolster the breeding program. The U. S. Fish and Wildlife Service has been reluctant to invoke the Endangered Species Act to force the necessary capture. Legal action has been started by the National Audubon Society and other groups to force officials to carry out their mandated duty. The ranchers apparently believe, naively in my opinion, that the birds will recover in the wild if left alone. However, the recent precipitous declines of Hawaiian Crows in surrounding areas suggest that it is only a matter of time until this last group disappears as well. Some so-called environmentalists have even suggested that the

crow should be allowed to die out "with dignity," as if the entire species is an ailing human individual on life-support. Because it is now a political football, Hawaii's only surviving crow, which might well have been saved, is probably doomed to rapid extinction. Hawaiian Crows tend to wander when not nesting, so it is still remotely possible for a birder to see one, but don't count on it. One was seen on Hualalai in 1991. The last accessible site where they could be seen regularly was the upper end of Kaloko Mauka Subdivision (Hawaii 7); the last sighting there was in 1983.

Japanese Bush-Warbler.
Originally confined to Oahu, the bush-warbler has recently spread to adjacent islands. Oahu remains the best place to hear (mostly) and see it. It is common in forest habitats throughout the island, as evidenced by its lovely song, but is very difficult to see unless one uses a tape recorded song playback. One locality where they are less shy is the Punamano Unit of James Campbell NWR (Oahu 12), where they may perch in the open on dead branches of haole koa along the main access road. On Kauai, they can be found in Keahua Arboretum (Kauai 1). They have become the most common bird in the forest of eastern Molokai such as in Kamakou Preserve (Molokai 2). Populations on Maui can be expected to increase dramatically in the coming years.

Elepaio. The populations of this native monarch flycatcher differ strikingly in plumage coloration among the three islands they inhabit. The possibility that they may prove to be three separate species cannot be discounted, although behaviorally all are very similar. Elepaio are still common on Hawaii and Kauai, but are now rare and apparently declining on Oahu. I know of no reliable locations for them on Oahu, but Aiea Ridge Trail (Oahu 16) would probably be the best place to look. The Kauai Elepaio is a conspicuous part of the avian community in all high-elevation forests such as at Kokee (Kauai 10) and in the Alakai Wilderness (Kauai 11). On the Big Island the birds vary so strongly from place to place that 3 subspecies have been recognized on that one island. The darkest forms are found in

Hawaii Volcanoes NP (Hawaii 2), particularly in Kipuka Ki on the Mauna Loa Road and at Thurston Lava Tube, and in Saddle Road kipukas (Hawaii 13). The pale mamane forest subspecies can be easily seen at Puu Laau (Hawaii 11). The intermediate Kona subspecies is less common but can be seen at Manuka State Park (Hawaii 4) and other nearby forests in South Kona Forest Reserve.

Kamao. In recent surveys, this extremely rare bird was found to be restricted to the very highest reaches of the Alakai Plateau, just below the peak of Waialeale (Kauai 11). A few individuals may still exist elsewhere, as indicated by several observations recently near the intersection of the Alakai Swamp and Pihea Ridge trails (Kauai 10).

Olomao. Possibly the rarest surviving native bird in Hawaii, this species clings to a precarious existence (if it is not already extinct) in the Kamakou Preserve (Molokai 2). It will probably be the next bird lost from Hawaii's native avifauna.

Omao. This is the only one of the native solitaires that can still be easily seen. It is a Big Island endemic and surprisingly has increased in numbers in the last decade. In Hawaii Volcanoes NP (Hawaii 2), look for it at Thurston Lava Tube, Kipuka Puaulu, and around Volcano House. Guests at this lodge are awakened by songs of Omao and Apapane. Omao are hard to see, but by

following their loud songs with a little patience you can usually get a good look. Early in the morning, an excellent vantage point is the balcony overlooking Kilauea Crater behind Volcano House where Omao sing from dead snags above the forest canopy and can be viewed from above. Omao are common in Hakalau Forest NWR (Hawaii 14) and in kipukas along the Saddle Road and Puu Oo Trail (Hawaii 13).

Puaiohi. Like its relative the Kamao, the Puaiohi is now vanishingly rare. The most recent sighting (1991) was along the trail to Koaie Stream from the end of Mohihi Rd. (Kauai 11). The further into the Alakai Wilderness you are able to get, the better your chances of finding this bird.

Greater Necklaced Laughing-thrush. This alien species is found only on Kauai where, because of its nomadic habits, it can be very elusive. The birds travel about in small flocks of up to 10 birds, and can turn up anywhere in lowland forest. No locality is totally reliable, but a few spots where the birds have turned up more than once include Keahua Arboretum (Kauai 1), Anahola Valley (Aliomanu Road) north of Kapaa, and Haiku Road which skirts Huleia NWR (Kauai 5). Look for them particularly between the end of the paved road and the stream. At Huleia, the birds may either be skulking in the dense understory or foraging quietly in the open crowns of the monkeypod and albizzia trees.

Melodious Laughing-thrush. Although this species is fairly common in lowland forests of several islands, and its song is loud and conspicuous, it is a very difficult bird to see except on Kauai where, for unknown reasons, it seems to be more likely to show itself in the open. It is frequently seen flying across the highway and on less travelled roads may sit on the shoulder. A good place to observe the latter phenomenon is Koolau Road, a loop of old highway bypassed by a newer stretch of Rt. 56 between Anahola and Kilauea. Watch for the road angling

sharply to the right at a fruit stand. The birds can even be seen in rather open areas along this road, which comes back into Rt. 56 nearer Kilauea. Melodious Laughing-thrushes can also be seen along Haiku Road (Kauai 5), along Aliomanu Road just north of the Anahola River, and at Haena Beach State Park (Kauai 4).

Red-billed Leiothrix. This species is rare and hard to find on Kauai and Oahu, but is fairly common in places on Maui and the Big Island. One of the best localities is the village of Kula on the lower slopes of Haleakala. Leiothrix live in thickets growing in gullies and ravines throughout the area, but can be hard to lure into view. They have become relatively tame and accustomed to people at Kula Botanical Gardens (admission charged). On the Big Island look for them along Mauna Loa Rd. and in Kipuka Puaulu in Hawaii Volcanoes NP (Hawaii 2). Another good locality is the Pohakuloa Section of Mauna Kea State Park (Hawaii 12) on the Saddle Road (Rt. 200).

Yellow-billed Cardinal. This species is quite common in kiawe thickets along the Kona coast of the Big Island. It even comes into open-air restaurants, such as the one at the Kona Bay Hotel, in Kailua-Kona. Other localities that are virtually certain to produce this species include Aimakapa Pond (Hawaii 6), Puuhonua o Honaunau NHP (City of Refuge) and Kealekekua Bay (Hawaii 5), and resort hotels along the Kohala coast south of Kawaihae (Hawaii 10).

Yellow-faced Grassquit. This small finch from Middle America is established in grassy areas of the northern Koolau Mountains, Oahu. The most reliable locality for it recently has been Manana Trail. To reach the trail, take Lunalilo Freeway (H-1) west (you can take a shortcut by following Moanalua Road (Rt. 78) instead of going by the airport but be sure you return to H-1 when the two intersect again) to Exit 10. Bear right on Moanalua Road to a T intersection at Waimano Home Road. Turn right (mauka) and watch carefully for the intersection of Komo Mai Drive (as is typical of Honolulu streets, the one sign is not easy to find and is not visible at all until the last second, so stay in the left lane) where you should turn left. Follow this street all the way to its end. The trail is beyond a gate at the end of the road. The first part is paved but it quickly narrows to a footpath. The grassquits can be in any grassy area along the trail, and sometimes can be seen in yards of the uppermost houses. The birds particularly like burned-over areas. Listen for their inconspicuous, grasshopperlike song, the key to finding this rather elusive alien.

Saffron Finch. This South American bird is now widespread and common in drier habitats of the Kohala and Kona regions of the Big Island, and can even be found around hotels in the Kailua-Kona area. It was thought to have died out on Oahu, but has been seen recently in the Salt Lake area (makai of Tripler Hospital).

Western Meadowlark. These birds are widespread and common in proper habitat in the Kauai lowlands. They are particularly conspicuous in fields along the main highway between Anahola and Kilauea and on mowed lawns and golf courses in Princeville. Other good spots include fields in lower Wailua Valley (Kauai 1) and dry habitats west of Kekaha.

Yellow-fronted Canary. On Oahu, this species is at present seen primarily in the Kapiolani Park area (Oahu 3). It is more widespread on the Big Island where it is found in a variety of forest and forest-edge habitats. It can be expected to spread throughout the island, so a sighting anywhere should not be considered unreasonable. Presently, the best sites are in the South Kohala-North Kona region (Hawaii 7, 8, and 11).

Ou. Early in the twentieth century this was one of the commonest Hawaiian native birds. Now whether it will survive to see the twenty-first is doubtful. It survived in fair numbers in Kauai's Alakai Swamp (Kauai 11) into the mid-1970s, but only two were found on a survey in 1989. A more recent unconfirmed sighting was along the Alakai Swamp Trail past Kawaikoi Stream (Kauai 10). On Hawaii, several populations were still present into the early 1980s. In 1984, a lava flow from Mauna Loa passed through the heart of the Ou's range, and only scattered sightings of this species have been made on Hawaii since then. The lava flow destroyed only a small part of the species' preferred habitat, so other factors are probably involved in the birds' disappearance. Of course, the main population may simply have moved to unoccupied habitat in an as-yet-undiscovered locality elsewhere, but no serious efforts have been made to search for them systematically. Here is a challenge for the intrepid birder willing to endure hikes over trackless lava flows into isolated kipukas, but it is strictly "at your own risk." Probably the best places to look would be in kipukas near the former population concentration as shown in *Forest Bird Communities of the Hawaiian Islands* (Scott *et al.* 1986; see "For Further Information").
You should obtain the U. S. Geological Survey map titled *Hawaii Volcanoes National Park and Vicinity, Hawaii*, on sale at the Volcano Observatory in the park (Detail Map P is based on this map, but for an Ou search you will need every detail). It shows the kipukas in detail and includes the most recent lava flows. In the late 1970s the few hundred Ou

were most densely concentrated in the area bounded by the Saddle Rd. on the north, the Kulani Tract on the south, and Powerline Road on the west. The Ou tended to range lower in elevation than other surviving native birds (which may have contributed to their decline), so the search should extend down to at least the 3500 ft. level. Another place to look would be the Olaa Tract, a disjunct wilderness area of the national park. Wright Road in the town of Volcano passes through a corner of this tract. One of the most recent Ou sightings was near the end of Wright Road. Unfortunately, no trails exist into Olaa and it is an area of very wet ohia forest with a dense tree-fern understory where one could easily get lost. Flagging tape would be very useful if you want to attempt the very difficult task of searching the Olaa Tract for Ou. Perhaps someone who reads this will rediscover a small population.

Palila. This species, the only finchlike Hawaiian honeycreeper the average birder is likely to see, lives above 7,000 feet in the mamane-naio forest belt around Mauna Kea on the Big Island. The densest concentration of birds is around Puu Laau (Hawaii 11), particularly above the cabin and to the right of the road looking mauka. There is some seasonal fluctuation as Palila wander to find green seed pods on the mamane trees. Even when present in numbers, they can be maddeningly quiet and difficult to locate. A more easily accessible spot, though far less reliable, is around the Onizuka Astronomy Complex on the paved road that leads to the observatories on Mauna Kea. This road is the only large paved road that heads toward Mauna Kea off the Saddle Rd. (Rt. 200). The intersection is at a prominent cinder cone, called Puu Huluhulu, on the south side of the Saddle Rd. The astronomy complex is a little over six miles from the intersection.

Maui Parrotbill. Until recently, everyone assumed that this endangered species could be seen only in the wilderness of East Maui (Maui 7), which remains the heart of the species' range. Fortunately for those unable to tackle a wilderness trek, parrotbills have recently (1989-91) been found in two relatively accessible spots in Waikamoi Preserve (Maui 5), one of which is traversed by the bird walks conducted regularly by staff members of Haleakala NP. Parrotbills were seen several times in 1990 in a large ravine that harbors a relict koa grove in the midst of the exotic trees of Hosmer Grove. The sightings included, at different times, both adult male and female and one immature male indicating the probable presence of a family group. Hopefully these birds and their progeny will provide the nucleus of a regularly accessible population. The other locality is further into the preserve, in the same area where Akohekohe are regularly seen along one of the old survey transects used by the Fish and Wildlife Service.

The services of a guide would be necessary to find the right spot. While at present no regular hikes are conducted to this site, that may change in the future. My own organized tours regularly visit the transect area, about an hour hike from the Hosmer Grove parking lot, and we sometimes allow birders not on the tour to accompany us. Contact the Nature Conservancy or Haleakala NP (addresses and phone numbers under site guides) for the most recent news of sightings and of upcoming guided visits to these localities. In light of the recent sightings in Waikamoi Preserve, birders at the Waikamoi Flume (Maui 6) should look for Maui Parrotbills. It is not very far away as the parrotbill flies.

Kauai Amakihi. Several researchers have recommended that this bird, considered a subspecies of Common Amakihi by the 1983 AOU Checklist, be given full species status. It is so regarded in *A Field Guide to the Birds of Hawaii and the Tropical Pacific*. Kauai Amakihi are common throughout the upland forests of the island. Easy places to see them include the hillside behind

the Kokee Museum and the overlooks at Kalalau Valley (Kauai 10). Photo by C. Fred Zeillemaker.

Common Amakihi. This is one of the few Hawaiian native birds that could be called "hard to miss." It ranges lower in elevation than most other Hawaiian honeycreepers and can even be found within a few minutes drive from downtown Honolulu (Oahu 1). It will be common in any locality where native birds occur, but the "amakihi capital of the world" must be Puu Laau (Hawaii 11) on the Big Island where they are abundant.

Anianiau. This Kauai endemic is common in all upper-elevation native forests on the island. In the Kokee area (Kauai 10), it outnumbers the Kauai Amakihi at the spots mentioned under that species.

Nukupuu. One of the "crown jewels" of Hawaiian birding, the Nukupuu is very elusive and has been seen by few living people. Nevertheless, it is probably more numerous than some other critically endangered species because the infrequent sightings are so widely scattered. Therein lies the problem for the birder; the sightings have not established any predictable pattern. The species survives only in the Alakai Swamp area (Kauai 11) and in the East Maui Wilderness (Maui 7). Sightings in Waikamoi Preserve (Maui 5) and in the Kokee area (Kauai 10) have not been confirmed and are probably based on misidentifications. Remember that the Kauai Amakihi has a *much longer and heavier bill* than the Common Amakihi. It is all too easy for birders accustomed to amakihi on other islands to let wishful thinking transform a Kauai Amakihi into a Nukupuu. An important point to remember is that the Nukupuu only rarely feeds on nectar. A bird feeding in flowers is likely to be an amakihi.

Akiapolaau. A Big Island endemic, this species has arguably the most bizarre bill of any passerine bird. Although endangered, the Akiapolaau is not so rare as some other native birds so classified, and most birders have a good chance of seeing one with a little effort. The biggest problem is that access to most of the montane koa-ohia forest favored by these birds is restricted. Probably the best place for the individual birder to try is Hakalau Forest NWR (Hawaii 14). The "Aki" can be found in kipukas along Puu Oo Trail and Powerline Road (Hawaii 13), but cannot be counted on. It also occurs in low numbers in mamane-naio forest around Puu Laau (Hawaii 11) but again is hard to find there. One of the best spots for the bird is the Kulani Correctional Facility, a minimum-security prison at the upper end of Stainback Hwy. Obviously, the prison is closed to the public (even the upper part of the access road is off-limits) but organized tour groups are sometimes allowed to visit. Such arrangements must be made at least 30 days in advance to allow for security clearance of all participants, and groups must be accompanied by someone familiar with the area. Another way to gain access to Kulani is to participate in the Volcano Christmas Bird Count. There is no guarantee that you will be on the Kulani team, but preferences are often given to those who have never been there. The compiler's address is published annually in *American Birds* (published by the National Audubon Society) and *'Elepaio* (published by Hawaii Audubon Society). [Note: The bird's name is a contraction of the Hawaiian phrase *'akihi-po'o-la'au* which means roughly "little green bird with a war club head" (*'akihi* = little green bird, *po'o* = head, *la'au* = war club) apparently in reference to the bird's woodpeckerlike feeding methods. There are irregular accents on the last three syllables: *ah-kee-ah-PO-LA-AU*. It's a tough one.]

Akikiki (Kauai Creeper). This Kauai endemic used to be fairly common in the Kokee area (Kauai 10) but is becoming increasingly difficult to find. The problem is confounded by the fact that these nuthatchlike birds are rather quiet and their rarely uttered song is very similar to that of the Kauai Amakihi. The most accessible area where the Akikiki has been seen regularly in recent years surrounds the Kawaikoi Stream (Kauai 10). The Alakai Swamp Trail (if you approach it from Camp 10 Road) provides the easiest access to the "good" area. Look for the birds anywhere beyond the intersection with Pihea Ridge Trail, but especially near the stream and across it. If you strike out here, return to the trail crossing and take the Kawaikoi Stream Trail to the left (it is the continuation of the Pihea Ridge Trail). This trail descends to the stream at a wider point and eventually brings you out on Camp 10 (Mohihi) Road. If the water is low, you can cross the stream at several points before you reach the road. Otherwise, you should turn left at the road and cross the stream at a concrete ford (expect to get your feet wet). Just up from the stream on the left another branch of Kawaikoi Stream Trail turns left into a planted grove of sugi trees (which look something like Monterey cypress). This is a beautiful and easy trail that parallels the stream and eventually dead-ends (most trail maps are a little confusing here). Look for Akikiki near the end of the trail. You can also reach this trail directly by just staying on the road past the Alakai Swamp Trail intersection. Of course, the further you can penetrate toward the Alakai Wilderness (Kauai 11), the better your chances of seeing an Akikiki.

Hawaii Creeper. This rather drab species is found in all the same areas as the Akiapolaau (which see) except for Puu Laau. However, the creeper is easier to find at Hakalau Forest NWR (Hawaii 14) than is the Aki. Occasionally, the Hawaii Creeper can be found in kipukas close by the Saddle Road (Hawaii 13).

Oahu Creeper (Oahu Alauahio). One of Hawaii's most elusive endangered species, this is Oahu's only endemic. Only a few sightings have been confirmed in the past two decades. Several of these were in North Halawa Valley, now being destroyed by freeway construction (see Island Swiftlet account). Oahu Creepers in the valley may have been wanderers from higher elevations, so a good place to look for them would be Aiea Ridge Trail (Oahu 16) above. Almost any trail that leads to the Koolau ridge could produce the creeper, but don't hold your breath.

Maui Creeper (Maui Alauahio). This Maui endemic is actually fairly common but is easily overlooked by the novice. The most accessible (and virtually 100% reliable) spot for it is Hosmer Grove in Haleakala National Park (Maui 4). To see them in numbers, try Polipoli Springs (Maui 8), Waikamoi Preserve (Maui 5), and Waikamoi Flume (Maui 6).

Akepa. For all practical purposes, this species survives only on the Big Island. The best place to see it is Hakalau Forest NWR (Hawaii 14) where it could almost be considered "hard to miss." It is much less numerous, but still regularly seen, at Kulani (see under Akiapolaau). Unfortunately, neither of these areas is readily accessible for the individual birder. A few Akepas inhabit forests on the northwestern slope of Hualalai, and, formerly at least, could be seen at the upper end of Kaloko Mauka Subdivision (Hawaii 7). They may still occasionally show up there, although the habitat is steadily deteriorating. They are also occasionally found in the Saddle Road kipukas (Hawaii 13), especially along Puu Oo Trail near its deadend at recent lava flows.

Akekee. In contrast to some other species, this Kauai endemic seems to have become easier to find in recent years. It is fairly common in the Kokee region (Kauai 10). It is almost always present around the Kalalau Valley overlooks and along Pihea Ridge Trail and is even seen regularly in the ohia trees in "Rooster Meadow" at Kokee Lodge. Check especially the trees between the picnic shelter and the campground. The Akekee is hard to miss along Camp 10 (Mohihi) Road and and associated trails. [Note: The 1983 AOU Check-list considered the Akekee a subspecies of Akepa, but in 1991 it was recognized as a full species.]

Iiwi. Although this species is still common, at least on Kauai, Maui, and Hawaii, it is not as widely distributed as other common honeycreepers. Iiwi can be seen easily in the Kokee area (Kauai 10), Hosmer Grove in Haleakala National Park (Maui 3), and in kipukas along the Saddle Road (Hawaii 13) on the Big Island. In Hawaii Volcanoes National Park (Hawaii 2), look for Iiwi at the upper end of Mauna Loa Road. In Kona, they are easily found in Kaloko Mauka Subdivision (Hawaii 7).

Akohekohe (Crested Honey-creeper). This spectacular bird is now known to be fairly common in the East Maui wilderness (Maui 7), but for most birders the best place to see it is Waikamoi Preserve (Maui 5) where it usually can be found with the aid of an experienced guide. The most reliable locality is a trail known informally as "Transect 7." It requires about an hour hike from the Hosmer Grove parking lot in Haleakala NP (Maui 4). Do not try to find this locality on your own. Waikamoi has a maze of trails, all of which look alike and are confusingly over-flagged. At present, the regularly organized hikes into Waikamoi do not visit the best locality for this species (although they sometimes find Akohekohe), but my own organized tours usually do and we sometimes allow outsiders to tag along. The Preserve Manager (for address, see Maui 5) will

know of any upcoming tours that might take you. Another locality that you can visit on your own is Waikamoi Flume (Maui 6). Because the flume has not been well worked by birders, I do not know how reliable it is for Akohekohe but they have definitely been seen there.

Apapane. This is the most abundant native bird in Hawaii, but tends to be more localized in distribution than the Common Amakihi. Where it occurs, it usually is abundant. Even casual tourists remark about the bright crimson birds they see from the balcony overlooking Kilauea Crater at Volcano House (Hawaii 2). Any locality that has ohia trees (and a few that do not, such as Puu Laau, Hawaii 11) will have Apapane.

Poo-uli. Few birders have any chance of seeing this bird. Its tiny range in the heart of the wilderness of East Maui (Maui 7) is now included in a natural area reserve and entry is controlled. See the Site Guide for further details.

Red-cheeked Cordonbleu. This introduced finch is very local. The birds can be very elusive because they often feed on the ground among tall dry grasses, when the only clue to their presence may be their easily overlooked thin *see-seee* call. When startled, the birds usually fly up and perch in low trees, where they may be more easily seen. The most reliable spot for them is the Puu Anahulu area (Hawaii 8). Look for the cordonbleu near the bottom of the hill where the road curves sharply within sight of the entrance road to Puu Waa Waa Ranch, as well as in Puu Lani Ranch subdivision. Another good place to look is west of the entrance to Puu Waa Waa Ranch along Mamalahoa Highway. Look for a large bulldozed area with a huge pile of rocks behind it on the mauka side of the road opposite a white-painted metal gate. You can park safely on the mauka side and bird either side of the road (the makai side is usually best, but I have seen the cordonbleu just behind the rock pile). Inside the fences is private land, however, and entering constitutes trespassing.

Lavender Waxbill. This species has nearly, if not entirely, disappeared from Oahu but seems to be increasing on the Big Island. They are usually present along the Mamalahoa Highway (Rt. 190) at Puu Anahulu (Hawaii 8). Look for them below the road where it traverses the side of a steep hill between Puu Waa Waa and Puu Lani Ranch. They are also found in residential areas of Kailua-Kona and at Puuhonua o Honaunau NHP (Hawaii 5).

Orange-cheeked Waxbill. The best locality by far for this waxbill is in Kaneohe (Oahu 8). Large flocks of this species as well as Common Waxbills, Nutmeg Mannikins, and Chestnut Mannikins inhabit patches of tall grass that border the Bay View Golf Center. To reach the best spot, turn onto Puohala Street directly in front of Castle High School on Kaneohe Bay Drive, then take the first right on Kulauli Street (there is a sign for Puohala Elementary School at the intersection). The street deadends at a water treatment plant. The waxbills can be anywhere in this area. Be sure to park on the public right-of-way (adjacent to the schoolyard is a good place) and bird from the road. Property owners have been very territorial here lately because of controversy over the area's future. The golf course wants to expand, but others want the land for a park. On Maui, Orange-cheeks can be found along Hansen Road between Puunene and the dump (Maui 1). Recently, they have been reported also in the Kihei area, so observers should be alert for them there. Orange-cheeks may be extirpated on the Big Island, but were seen at Puu Anahulu (Hawaii 8) within the last decade.

Black-rumped Waxbill. Probably the most elusive of the introduced estrildids in Hawaii, this species is now found only on the Big Island. The birds move around in flocks as they search for grasses at the proper stage of seed production. Thus they are unpredictable. All observations recently have been in the South Kohala-North Kona region, including Puu Anahulu (Hawaii 8). At that locality, they can be seen on the steep hillside along the main highway or in weedy parts of Puu Lani Ranch subdivision. Look for them mixed in with flocks of Red Avadavats.

Common Waxbill. This species is now widespread on Oahu. They are common in grassy or weedy places near Kahuku (Oahu 11), along the road leading into the Honouliuli Unit of Pearl Harbor NWR (Oahu 15), and at Bay View Golf Center in Kaneohe (see directions under Orange-cheeked Waxbill). Less often, they may be seen in the mauka part of Kapiolani Park (Oahu 3) behind the archery range and tennis courts.

Red Avadavat. For years this bird had been known in Hawaii and elsewhere by the lovely and appropriate name "Strawberry Finch." However, the 1983 AOU Check-list opted instead for this name, which no one seems to know how to pronounce, so we are stuck with it. For nearly half a century after they were introduced, Red Avadavats were found only in the immediate vicinity of Pearl Harbor. Now they have spread nearly throughout Oahu, but Pearl Harbor remains their stronghold. Look for them in the edges of sugar cane fields. They are often seen at James Campbell NWR (Oahu 11) and around Waialua (Oahu 14). They are also well established in North Kona and South Kohala on the Big Island where they roam about in large flocks. They can usually be found at Puu Anahulu (Hawaii 8). [Note: According to *The Random House Dictionary of the English Language*, Second Edition, "avadavat" is pronounced with a heavy accent on the first syllable and a secondary one on the last: *AH-vah-dah-VAHT*. Try to avoid the tendency to make it sound like "abba-dabba."]

Warbling Silverbill. This is now the most abundant of the estrildid finches in the North Kona-South Kohala region of the Big Island, and is not confined to that area. Expect it in any dry habitat on Hawaii. On Maui, silverbills are common in the central isthmus and in the Kihei area. They are much less common on Oahu, where most sightings are on the dry southeastern end between Hawaii Kai and Makapuu.

Chestnut Mannikin. This is the most common estrildid on Kauai where huge flocks resembling swarms of bees can sometimes be seen. They are particularly abundant in the grassy edges of sugar cane fields, but you may find them in the grass bordering the entrance loop at Lihue Airport or on the lawn of your hotel. On Oahu, they are common in the central valley from Pearl Harbor to Haleiwa, along the North Shore, and in the Kahuku area.

FOR FURTHER INFORMATION

This annotated bibliography lists references in a variety of categories. Because most birders are at least passingly interested in other aspects of natural history, titles that deal with plants, geology, other terrestrial vertebrates, underwater life, and general natural history are given in addition to bird references. No one can really enjoy birds in Hawaii without at least a little knowledge of their environment. Comments are given under some references to guide you in doing your "homework" or in choosing reference materials for a trip. This list is not comprehensive, and reflects the author's attitude and experience. Undoubtedly, some worthy publications have been overlooked; I apologize to any authors so slighted.

Birds

AMERICAN ORNITHOLOGISTS' UNION (AOU). 1983. *Check-list of North American Birds.* 6th. Ed. Washington, D. C.: American Ornithologists' Union. [This is the definitive reference for both English and scientific names of birds in North America, and it now includes the Hawaiian Islands. Revisions to the check-list are published annually in the July issue of *The Auk*, journal of the AOU.]

BERGER, ANDREW J. 1981. *Hawaiian Birdlife.* 2nd. Ed. Univ. of Hawaii Press, Honolulu. [The standard home reference "state bird book." Includes quotations from much older literature that make fascinating reading. After the field guides, the book birders should consult most frequently.]

HARRISON, CRAIG S. 1990. *Seabirds of Hawaii: Natural History and Conservation.* Cornell Univ. Press, Ithaca and London.

HARRISON, PETER. 1983. *Seabirds: an Identification Guide.* Boston: Houghton Mifflin Co. [A worldwide reference. Seabirds are great wanderers and almost any species could show up in Hawaiian waters, so this is a useful backup to a Hawaii field guide. More detailed than the following title. Illustrated with color paintings.]

HARRISON, PETER. 1987. *A Field Guide to Seabirds of the World.* Lexington, MA: The Stephen Greene Press. [A smaller and more portable guide by the previous author. Illustrated with photographs.]

HAWAII AUDUBON SOCIETY. 1989. *Hawaii's Birds.* 4th. Ed. Honolulu: Hawaii Audubon Society. [A pocket-size reference that has been the workhorse field guide in Hawaii for decades. Newly updated. Illustrated mostly with photographs. Widely available in Hawaii or by mail directly from the Society.]

HAYMAN, PETER, JOHN MARCHANT, and TONY PRATER. 1986. *Shorebirds: An identification guide to the waders of the world.* Boston: Houghton Mifflin Co. [A definitive, well-illustrated reference. Anyone looking for rare shorebirds in Hawaii should have it.]

MADGE, STEVE, and HILARY BURN. 1988. *Waterfowl: An identification guide to the ducks, geese, and swans of the world.* Boston: Houghton Mifflin Co. [Another of the recent world field guides very useful in Hawaii because of the potential for rare ducks to show up. British edition titled *Wildfowl* and published by Christopher Helm.]

NATIONAL GEOGRAPHIC SOCIETY. 1987. *Field Guide to the Birds of North America.* 2nd. Ed. Washington, D. C.: National Geographic Society. [A handy quick reference for seabirds, shorebirds, and waterfowl that migrate to Hawaii. Easier to pack in the field than other references to these groups. Obtainable from the Society or nonprofit sources such as the visitor center at Kilauea Point NWR or the American Birding Association.]

PRATT, H. DOUGLAS, PHILLIP L. BRUNER, and DELWYN G. BERRETT. 1987. *A Field Guide to the Birds of Hawaii and the Tropical Pacific.* Princeton, N. J.: Princeton Univ. Press. [The only field guide to illustrate all Hawaiian birds, in color plates by Pratt. Sponsored by Hawaii Audubon Society and more detailed than *Hawaii's Birds*; the two are complementary.]

PYLE, ROBERT L. 1988. Checklist of the Birds of Hawaii - 1988. *'Elepaio* 48: 95-106. [The "official" state checklist. Available for $2.00 from Hawaii Audubon Society, P. O. Box 22832, Honolulu HI 96822.]

PYLE, ROBERT L. and ANDREW ENGILIS, JR. 1987. *Field Check-card of Birds of Hawaii.* Hawaii Audubon Society, Honolulu. [A pocket-size checklist available from the Society, P. O. Box 22832, Honolulu HI 96822.]

SCOTT, J. MICHAEL, STEPHEN MOUNTAINSPRING, FRED L. RAMSEY, and CAMERON B. KEPLER. 1986. Forest bird communities of the Hawaiian Islands: Their dynamics, ecology, and conservation. *Studies in Avian Biology No. 9.* [A highly technical work that reports the results of the epic population surveys of Hawaiian birds conducted by the U. S. Fish and Wildlife Service during the late 1970s. Indispensable for anyone wishing to seek out the rarest of the rare. Available at the main visitor center, Hawaii Volcanoes National Park.]

Mammals, Reptiles, and Amphibians

KAUFMAN, G. D., and P. H. FORESTELL. 1986. *Hawaii's Humpback Whales.* Kihei, HI: Pacific Whale Foundation Press. [Everything you always wanted to know about humpbacks.]

MCKEOWN, SEAN. 1978. *Hawaiian Reptiles and Amphibians.* Honolulu: Oriental Publishing Co. [A widely available guide with excellent photographs.]

MINASIAN, S. M., K. C. BALCOMB III, and L. FOSTER. 1987. *The Whales of Hawaii.* San Francisco: The Marine Mammal Fund. [A guide to all species of marine mammals in Hawaii.]

SCOTT, SUSAN. 1988. *Oceanwatcher: an Above-water Guide to Hawaii's Marine Animals.* Honolulu: Green Turtle Press. [Includes seabirds.]

TOMICH, P. QUENTIN. 1986. *Mammals in Hawai'i* 2nd. Ed. Honolulu: Bishop Museum Press. [The standard library reference.]

VAN RIPER, SANDRA G., and CHARLES VAN RIPER III. 1982. *A Field Guide to the Mammals in Hawaii.* Honolulu: Oriental Publishing Co. [The best guide for field use.]

Plants

HARGREAVES, D. and B. HARGREAVES. 1964. *Tropical Trees of Hawaii.* Kailua, HI: Hargreaves Co. [A photographic guide to mainly introduced trees seen around towns.]

KEPLER, ANGELA KAY. 1983. *Hawaiian Heritage Plants.* Honolulu: Oriental Publishing Co. [An excellent guide to plants of significance to the history of Hawaii.]

KEPLER, ANGELA KAY. 1990. *Trees of Hawai'i.* Honolulu: University of Hawaii Press. [Good photographic coverage of native and introduced trees.]

LAMB, SAMUEL H. 1981. *Native Trees and Shrubs of the Hawaiian Islands.* Santa Fe, NM: The Sunstone Press.

LAMOUREUX, CHARLES H. 1976. *Trailside Plants of Hawaii's National Parks.* Hawaii Volcanoes National Park: Hawaii Natural History Association. [Small and spiral bound, photographically illustrated. Useful in any forest area on Maui or Hawaii.]

MERLIN, MARK DAVID. 1976. *Hawaiian Forest Plants.* Honolulu: Oriental Publishing Co. [The best of the small popular guides.]

MERLIN, MARK DAVID. Undated. *Hawaiian Coastal Plants and Scenic Shorelines.* Honolulu: Oriental Publishing Co.

PERRY, F., and R. HAY. 1982. *A Field Guide to Tropical and Subtropical Plants.* New York: Van Nostrand Reinhold Co. [Covers plants widely planted throughout the world's tropical regions, including Hawaii.]

ROCK, JOSEPH F. 1974. *The Indigenous Trees of the Hawaiian Islands.* Rutland, Vt. and Tokyo: Charles E. Tuttle Co. [First published in 1913, this remains the standard reference on the subject.]

SOHMER, S. H., and ROBERT GUSTAFSON. 1987. *Plants and Flowers of Hawai'i.* Honolulu: Univ. of Hawaii Press. [A wonderfully well written and well illustrated new book. Not exactly a field guide, but recommended to anyone interested in native plant communities.]

Underwater Life

CARPENTER, R. B., and B. C. CARPENTER. 1981. *Fish Watching in Hawaii.* San Mateo, CA: Natural World Press.

FIELDING, ANN. 1979. *Hawaiian Reefs and Tidepools.* Honolulu: Oriental Publishing Co.

FIELDING, ANN, and E. ROBINSON. 1987. *An Underwater Guide to Hawai'i.* Honolulu: Univ. of Hawaii Press.

GOODSON, GAR. 1973. *The Many-splendored Fishes of Hawaii.* Palos Verdes Estates, CA: Marquest Colorguide Books. [A popular and useful small guide. Widely available in Hawaii.]

RANDALL, JOHN E. 1981. *Underwater Guide to Hawaiian Reef Fishes.* Newtown Square, Pa.: Harrowood Books. [Printed on plastic, can be taken underwater. Illustrated with photographs.]

TINKER, SPENCER W. 1978. *Fishes of Hawaii: a Handbook of the Marine Fishes of Hawaii and the Central Pacific Ocean.* Honolulu: Hawaiian Services, Inc. [The standard library reference.]

Geology, Geography, and Archaeology

ARMSTRONG, R. W., Ed. 1983. *Atlas of Hawaii,* 2nd. Ed. Honolulu: Univ. of Hawaii Press. [An excellent reference that contains far more than basic maps.]

COX, J. H., and E. STASACK. 1970. *Hawaiian Petroglyphs.* Honolulu: Bishop Museum Press.

DECKER, BARBARA and ROBERT. 1986. *Road Guide to Hawaii Volcanoes National Park.* Mariposa, CA: Double Decker Press. [Includes excellent detail maps of most places birders are likely to visit.]

DECKER, ROBERT and BARBARA. 1980. *Volcano Watching.* Hawaii Volcanoes National Park: Hawaii Natural History Association.

FRIERSON, PAMELA. 1991. *The Burning Island: A Journey through Myth and History in Volcano Country, Hawai'i.* San Francisco: Sierra Club Books.

JENNINGS, JESSE D. 1979. *The Prehistory of Polynesia.* Cambridge, MA: Harvard Univ. Press.

MACDONALD, GORDON A., AGATIN T. ABBOTT, and FRANK L. PETERSON. 1983. *Volcanoes in the Sea: the Geology of Hawaii.* Honolulu: Univ. of Hawaii Press.

MACDONALD, GORDON A., and DOUGLASS H. HUBBARD. 1973. *Volcanoes of the National Parks in Hawaii.* 6th. Ed. Hawaii Volcanoes National Park: Hawaii Natural History Association.

STEARNS, HAROLD T. 1985. *Geology of the State of Hawaii.* 2nd. Ed. Palo Alto, CA: Pacific Books, Publishers.

General Natural History

CARLQUIST, SHERWIN. 1980. *Hawaii: a Natural History*, 2nd. Ed. Lawai, HI: Pacific Tropical Botanical Garden. [A classic general reference with a botanical bias. Taxonomy, especially of birds, now outdated but still a useful and interesting book.]

CULLINEY, JOHN L. 1988. *Islands in a Far Sea: Nature and Man in Hawaii*. San Francisco: Sierra Club Books. [An excellent book that should be read by anyone interested in Hawaiian natural history and conservation.]

KEPLER, ANGELA KAY. 1987. *Maui's Hana Highway: a Visitor's Guide*. Honolulu: Mutual Publishing Co.

KEPLER, CAMERON B. and ANGELA KAY KEPLER. 1988. *Haleakala: a Guide to the Mountain*. Honolulu: Mutual Publishing Co.

MITCHELL, ANDREW. 1990. *The Fragile South Pacific: an Ecological Odyssey*. Univ. Texas Press, Austin. [Covers the entire South Pacific and helps to place the Hawaiian Islands in proper ecological perspective.]

STONE, CHARLES P., and DANIELLE B. STONE, Eds. *Conservation Biology in Hawai'i*. Honolulu: Univ. of Hawaii Cooperative National Park Resources Studies Unit.

Appendix
PICTORIAL GUIDE TO PLANTS
MENTIONED IN THIS GUIDE

Banana poka *Passiflora molissima*

Beach naupaka *Scaevola taccada*

Blackberry *Rubus penetrans*

Black wattle *Acacia decurrens*

Breadfruit *Artocarpus incisus*

Fountain Grass *Pennisetum setaceum*

Eucalyptus (swamp
mahogany) *Eucalyptus
robusta*

Guava *Psidium guajava*

Halapepe *Pleomele aurea*

Haleakala sandalwood
Santalum haleakalae

Haole koa *Leucaena leucocephala*

Ieie *Freycinetia arborea*

Hapuu *Cibotium glaucum*

Ironwood "cones"

Ironwood *Casuarina equisetifolia*
with Fairy Tern

Jacaranda *Jacaranda mimosaefolia*

Kiawe (algoroba) *Prosopis
pallida*

Koa *Acacia koa*

Koa "parkland"

Kukui (candlenut) *Aleurites
moluccana*

Lama *Diospyros ferrea*

Mamane *Sophora chrysophylla*

Lilikoi (passionfruit) *Passiflora sp.*

Mango *Mangifera indica*

Mamane flowers

Monkeypod *Samanea saman*

Mountain apple *Eugenia malaccensis*

Red ohia flowers

Naio *Myoporum sandwicense*

Yellow ohia flowers

Ohia-lehua *Metrosideros collina*

Ohia terminal leaf buds

Pilo *Coprosma montana*

Silversword *Argyroxiphium sandwicense*

Silk oak *Grevillea rubusta*

Taro *Colocasia esculenta*

Silver geranium *Geranium cuneatum*

Wiliwili *Erythrina sandwicensis*

Wiliwili flowers

Wiliwili haole *Erythrina indica*

Index